Bands as Virtual Organisations

Electronic Business

Herausgegeben von Christine Strauss

Band 8

PETER LANG

Frankfurt am Main · Berlin · Bern · Bruxelles · New York · Oxford · Wien

Christine Bauer

Bands as Virtual Organisations

Improving the Processes of Band
and Event Management with Information
and Communication Technologies

PETER LANG
Internationaler Verlag der Wissenschaften

Bibliographic Information published by the Deutsche Nationalbibliothek
The Deutsche Nationalbibliothek lists this publication in the Deutsche Nationalbibliografie; detailed bibliographic data is available in the internet at http://dnb.d-nb.de.

Cover design:
© Olaf Glöckler, Atelier Platen, Friedberg

Printed with financial support
of the Austrian Research Association, Vienna.

ISSN 1868-646X
ISBN 978-3-631-63057-0
© Peter Lang GmbH
Internationaler Verlag der Wissenschaften
Frankfurt am Main 2012
All rights reserved.

All parts of this publication are protected by copyright. Any utilisation outside the strict limits of the copyright law, without the permission of the publisher, is forbidden and liable to prosecution. This applies in particular to reproductions, translations, microfilming, and storage and processing in electronic retrieval systems.
www.peterlang.de

"Don't be scared
to fly alone,
find a path that is your own."

(in the song "Soar", words & music by Christina Aguilera,
Robert D. Hoffman, & Heather Noelle Holley)

Acknowledgements

I could never have succeeded without the help, support, and guidance of a lot of people.

Through my academic career, many people have helped me accomplish both my short and long-term goals. I would like to express my sincere appreciation and gratitude to those who believe in me. It is these people who have given me the strength to keep moving.

My dearest thanks go to Gerald Seilinger for sharing his knowledge of the processes in music business. He provided me with detailed insider information on his work. Thanks for giving me the chance to be part of your *roadie* and *advisor* team, Gerald.

Furthermore I would like to thank ao. Univ.-Prof. Mag. Dr. Christine Strauss for her support and encouragement throughout my scientific work. She offered valuable assistance and guidance. Above all, she showed me to trust my interests and encouraged me to sing my own song.

Special thanks go to Jürgen Mangler for inspiring my interest in informatics. I still remember the evening when he showed me how to use Vi(m) and do Perl scripting. Who knows if I would have ever started to study business informatics without that evening.

Above all I want to thank my parents and family for all their love and support. Without them, I would not be where I am.

Abstract

Managing a big band is a challenge, similar to managing a small or medium-sized enterprise. A type of band particularly difficult to manage is a *telephone band* that does not have a fixed line-up of musicians. Together, the musicians form a virtual organisation with the bandleader as a focal company. Every participant in the organisation brings in a certain set of skills, has specific business goals, and has to bear some risks. The focal company has to assume full contractual liability to the event organiser. However, bandleaders managing these organisational constructs typically have an artistic background rather than a managerial one.

To date, the processes involved in managing bands have not been analysed. It is nearly impossible to improve these processes because processes are not clear. In a competitive environment, members do not seek to share knowledge on processes with their competitors because knowledge on processes is a business asset. However, as virtual organisations, musicians and bandleaders are mutually dependent. Accordingly, knowledge sharing forms the basis for process improvements, which can only be achieved by joint efforts.

Accordingly, this work delivers results in the following areas. First, this investigation targets the activities involved in managing a medium-sized *telephone band*, made transparent by modelling the processes. Second, this work analyses the resulting models and suggests points for improvement with particular emphasis on the adoption of information and communication technologies.

Due to the case study's explorative nature, using qualitative research methods appears to be the most appropriate alternative in this context. Data is collected through a semi-structured interview and direct participant-observation. Findings are modelled adhering to the UML (Unified Modeling Language) notation for activity diagrams. For deriving implications and suggestions for process improvement, a SWOT (strengths, weaknesses, opportunities, threats) analysis is performed.

This study's major findings include a thorough documentation of processes, making tacit knowledge explicit. Emphasising the use of ICT (information and communication technologies), the findings provide a chronological sequence of activities that may be generalised to band and event management.

Contents

I	Figures	XIII
II	Tables	XV
III	Abbreviations	XVII

1.	Motivation and problem definition	1
1.1	Objectives	2
1.2	Relevance	3
1.3	Structure	5
1.4	Remarks	7
2.	Theory and reference frame	9
2.1	Artists and artisans	9
2.2	The definition of a band	12
2.3	Music management: The musician as one-person enterprise	14
2.4	The *telephone band* as a virtual organisation	15
3.	Methods	21
3.1	The research approach	21
	3.1.1 The research strategy	22
	3.1.2 The study design	26
	3.1.2.1 The case study as a research strategy	29
	3.1.2.2 The case study design	32
3.2	Language definition for the visualisation of processes	40
3.3	Instruments of evaluation	42
4.	Case study	47
4.1	Current situation – process model	48

4.1.1 Initiation and pre-event planning	48
4.1.2 Pre-event execution on the day of the event	55
4.1.3 Execution: performing at the event	57
4.1.4 Post-event activities and closing	57
4.2 SWOT analysis	61
4.2.1 Evaluation	61
4.2.2 Strategy development	64
4.3 Suggestions for improvements with particular consideration to information and communication technologies	65
4.3.1 Organising the timetable	68
4.3.2 Installing and dismantling stage equipment	69
4.3.3 Organising musicians	70
4.3.4 Organising rehearsals	74
4.3.5 Organising sheet music	75
4.3.6 Creating the set list and submitting the song list to the collecting society	76
4.3.7 Providing payment	78
4.3.8 Final check at the venue	80
5. Discussion and outlook	83
5.1 Interpretation of results	83
5.2 Future research	85
6. Summary	89
7. References	91
Appendix	101

I Figures

Figure 1. Structure and dependencies among sections of this work 6
Figure 2. Frequency of research method use in the journal "Wirtschaftsinformatik" (business and information systems engineering) 28
Figure 3. Case study research design 31
Figure 4. Quick reference for UML activity diagram notation according to UML 2.3 41
Figure 5. The four SWOT dimensions 43
Figure 6. Matrix representation of the SWOT analysis 44
Figure 7. UML activity diagram for the performance at the event 49
Figure 8. UML activity diagram for organising the musicians for VBO 50
Figure 9. UML activity diagram for organising sheet music 52
Figure 10. UML activity diagram for organising rehearsals 54
Figure 11. UML activity diagram for handling the installation on stage 56
Figure 12. UML activity diagram for providing payment 58
Figure 13. UML activity diagram for handling the dismantlement of stage equipment 59
Figure 14. UML activity diagram for performing the final check 60
Figure 15. UML activity diagram for the improved process of performing at the event 66
Figure 16. UML activity diagram for organising the timetable 69
Figure 17. UML activity diagram for the improved process of handling the installation on stage 71
Figure 18. UML activity diagram for the improved process of handling the dismantlement of stage equipment 72
Figure 19. UML activity diagram for the improved process for organising musicians 73
Figure 20. Entity relationship diagram for the song database 77
Figure 21. UML activity diagram for preparing fee notes 78
Figure 22. UML activity diagram for improving the process of payment 80

II Tables

Table 1. From artist and artisan as synonyms to the separation of qualities 10
Table 2. Relevant situations for different research strategies 23
Table 3. Selecting the research strategy 27
Table 4. A comparison of case study with experimental and survey approaches 30
Table 5. SWOT matrix for the event organisation 62

III Abbreviations

AKM	Autoren, Komponisten, Musikverleger, an Austrian collecting society
BPMN	Business Process Modeling Notation
cf.	confer, the Latin phrase for *compare*
etc.	et cetera, the Latin phrase for *and so on*
i.e.	id est. the Latin phrase for *that is*
ICT	information and communication technologies
N. N.	nomen nescio, the Latin phrase for an unknown person
PEST	political, economic, social, technological
PoC	push-to-talk over cellular
PTT	push-to-talk
RFID	radio frequency identification
SME	small or medium-sized enterprise
SO	strengths, opportunities
ST	strengths, threats
SWOT	strengths, weaknesses, opportunities, threats
TOWS	threats, opportunities, weaknesses, strengths (cf. SWOT)
UML	Unified Modeling Language
USP	unique selling proposition
VAT	value-added tax
VBO	Vienna Ballroom Orchestra
VoIP	Voice-over Internet protocol
vs.	versus
WO	weaknesses, opportunities
WT	weaknesses, threats

1. Motivation and problem definition

Managing the members of a music group as large as a big band or even an orchestra is a challenging task. In terms of general infrastructure and the number of people involved, a band or orchestra can be compared to a small or medium-sized enterprise (SME) (O'del, 2003). Usually, though, bandleaders and conductors managing these bands have an artistic education and perceive themselves as artists rather than band managers. Thus, it does not come as a surprise that bandleaders, as most artists, lack any kind of business or managerial education (e.g., Bauer, Viola, & Strauss, 2011; Bolan, 2002; Eikhof & Haunschild, 2007; Menger, 1999; O'del, 2003; Røyseng, Mangset, & Borgen, 2007; Viola, 2009).

Still, for centuries, bandleaders have been able to manage their bands and orchestras (Ginsburgh & Throsby, 2006, p. 139; North, 1996, pp. 32-33) without the assistance of any management experts. They acquired, learned, and developed their knowledge and skills by asking colleagues, observing and imitating other professionals in their environments, and ultimately learning by doing (Fenderich, 2005).

However, the processes that bandleaders currently follow in managing their bands are not clear. While research on organisations, group behaviour, and process modelling are extensive and delve into almost any conceivable academic domain, studies in the field of arts, and particularly music management, are still scarce (e.g., Bauer, et al., 2011; Fink, 1996; Gensch, Stöckler, & Tschmuck, 2009; Moussetis & Ernst, 2004; Tschmuck, 2003, 2008; Viola, 2009; Weaver & Bowman, 2005). Yet, the *how to's* of band managing seem to be insider information that every artist and bandleaders only share within their microcosms.

Literature that exist in this field mostly targets practitioners (e.g., Frascogna & Hetherington, 2004; Röttgers, 2003) and either focuses on marketing aspects (e.g., Lathrop & Pettigrew, 2003; Röttgers, 2003) or describes the market structure in global or generic terms (e.g., Clement, Papies, & Schusser, 2008; Kulle, 1998; Schneider & Weinacht, 2007; Tschmuck, 2003).

To date, the processes have neither been analysed by researchers nor taught at arts and/or business schools (Bauer, et al., 2011; O'del, 2003; Viola, 2009). It is still unclear which processes are involved in managing a band and whether these processes can be improved, and even if they can be improved, whether bandleaders perform well without any specific management training.

A specific type of band to be managed is – in musicians' jargon – a *telephone band* (N. N., 2008; Strunk, 2006). A *telephone band* does not have a fixed line-up (i.e. the band members are not set or permanent); instead, musicians are only included in the band for a specific performance (e.g., concert, ball, event, *gig*).

A *telephone band* is comparable to a virtual organisation, where independent organisations share resources to achieve a common goal. Every musician in the band acts as a one-person enterprise (i.e. an enterprise where the only consistent staff member is the business owner him or herself). The bandleader, also a one-person enterprise, acts as the focal organisation (i.e. the organisation linking customer requirements to inbound and outbound activities of the participating enterprises). Every participant in the virtual organisation brings in certain skills and knowledge that are required in the organisation. Furthermore, each one-person enterprise pursues its specific business goals and simultaneously has to bear certain risks.

Scenarios where big companies cooperate as virtual organisations rarely occur. Accordingly, it is difficult to observe and research such constructs on a large basis. *Telephone bands*, in contrast, are a rather frequent phenomenon in the *non-superstar music business* (commercial music). Accordingly, this domain suggests itself for the investigation of virtual organisations. As a consequence, this work concentrates on this hardly researched field. Furthermore, coordinating larger bands is a more complex task than coordinating smaller bands. Because managing a large band inevitably makes it easier to manage a small band, this work focuses on larger bands, particularly *telephone big bands*.

1.1 Objectives

This work aims to deliver results in the following fields:

- First, the research targets the processes and activities involved in managing a medium-sized *telephone band* or orchestra by defining them and making them transparent (i.e., modelling the processes). The processes and activities are analysed and illustrated based on a case study.

- Second, this work analyses the resulting models and reveals points for improvement.

- Third, it suggests specific opportunities for improvements (solutions), particularly with the use of information and communication technologies (ICT).

- Fourth, with the discussion of a case study, the research documents the activities and builds the basis for professionals' activities in transferring the findings to similar situations.

This research is interdisciplinary in its core. It considers strategic elements for managing virtual organisations (management science). The discussion of the case study focuses on the domain of arts (arts and cultural sciences). Here, a specific occurrence of a virtual organisation is analysed: bandleaders managing their bands and orchestras, i.e., groups (social sciences). Therefore, involved processes are visualised using standardised models as they occur in computer science and operations research. Finally, the research suggests improvements with particular view to the application of information and communication technologies (business informatics).

Essentially, this research targets three major groups of readers:

- First, results will help bandleader aspirants and current professionals in acquiring and developing specific knowledge *and relevant* skills for their (future) jobs.

- Second, this work will present a sound basis for the further investigations of other researchers and should encourage researchers to consider an interdisciplinary view in research.

- Third, results should inspire and guide educators and curricula developers in higher education, in regards to what bandleaders need to know in doing and improving their jobs and subsequently, what contents should be included in curricula and syllabi.

1.2 Relevance

As already indicated in the section above, this work targets both scientists as well as practitioners.

Scientific relevance

This work's scientific relevance is twofold. It contributes to the research on virtual organisations but is also relevant for music management.

Starting in the early 1990s, the development of advanced ICT was one of the main drivers that enabled virtual organisations. Researchers envisioned large networks of organisations collaborating as virtual organisations, based on trust. Soon researchers discovered that such organisations did not emerge as frequently as they desired for researching the phenomenon: Large companies rarely cooperate as virtual organisations, and SMEs tend to need lobbying activities to engage in such cooperation (for details on SME networks cf. Haas, 2007).

In the music business, however, professional musicians – as one-person enterprises – frequently cooperate as *telephone bands*, on a level that we consider virtual organisations (cf. Section 2.4). They form bands for specific events but part ways afterwards. The formation processes in this business are fast moving and occur more frequently than virtual organisations where large-scale companies cooperate. Hence, *telephone bands* offer a good opportunity for research on virtual organisations.

However, the music business is not as transparent as other business fields. For decades, music was looked at from an artistic or cultural perspective, while its economic or managerial perspective was neglected. Only recently have researchers started taking an interest in music management, meaning it is a young domain that lacks fundamental research.

Processes are not transparent and have not really been researched as of yet. Knowledge on processes is tacit knowledge. Outsiders and newcomers in the music business cannot necessarily pinpoint individuals' processes for managing bands because of this lack of research and knowledge sharing. Without research, improving these processes is near impossible, particularly when it comes to adopting new technologies.

Introducing a business informatics view with its specific approaches, methods, and findings from other fields of applications to the domain of music management will bring new insights to the (growing) music management community as well as to the larger groups of scientists in cultural management, general management, and – last but not least – business informatics.

Since this research field is interdisciplinary, results are relevant to researchers in business informatics and information systems, management science, social sciences, and cultural sciences (in particular musicology).

Practical relevance

Since management scenarios of bandleaders for *telephone bands* are analysed in a case study, this research is significant for people acting as bandleaders in any kind of musical group without a fixed line-up. As the study is carried out in context of a big band, findings will be of particular interest for bandleaders in this field. Additionally, major parts of this research are also relevant for smaller *telephone bands* and for fixed-member music groups of any size.

Beyond its pertinence in the music business, findings on ICT-support of processes are also relevant for any kind of event organisation. Small events such as company parties involve processes similar to big events such as the Olympic games. In any kind of event management project, people need to be coordinated, dates have to be fixed, the venue has to be set-up and decorated as well deconstructed afterwards, etc. Tools supporting *telephone bands* may thus also be applicable for the management of events and virtual organisations.

1.3 Structure

Figure 1 outlines the structure of this work. Arrows connect sections with the other sections that they depend on. A dashed-lined arrow indicates that the respectively referenced section is used; this applies for the references and the appendix. Generally, the dependencies among sections are transitive, which means that Section 3 (Methods) is not only connected to Section 2 (Theory and reference frame) but also to Section 1 (Motivation and problem definition).

This work starts with a motivation and problem definition (Section 1). Practitioners may prefer to go directly to Section 4 (Case study). Scientists and interested readers are introduced to this work's theory and framing (Section 2); this section makes use of references to literature, which is listed in Section 7. Section 3 discusses the methodologies used in this work. The results' discussion and outlook to future research will be particularly interesting for scientists (Section 5). Finally, this work concludes with a summary (Section 6).

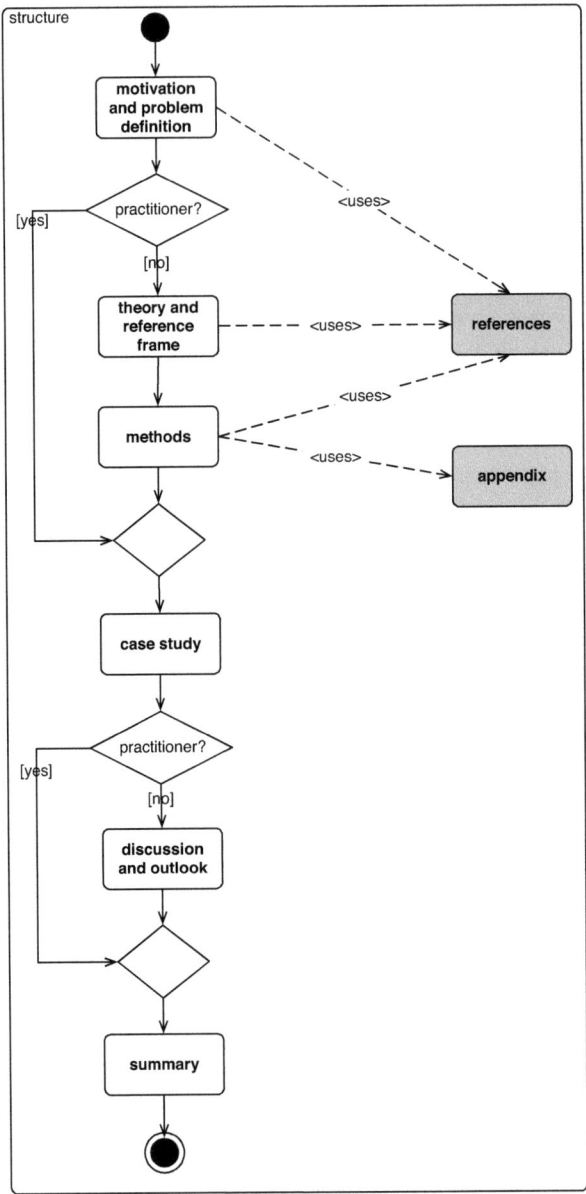

Figure 1. Structure and dependencies among sections of this work

Basically, Figure 1 illustrates the sections' interdependencies in terms of train of thoughts (i.e., ideas and elaborations of one section flow into another). However, these dependencies are not intended to convey mandatory reading instructions but should rather guide the reader through the work.

The appendix includes the questionnaire, which was used as guide for the semi-structured interview, in German with English translations.

1.4 Remarks

- References are cited by author name(s) and year of publication within the text, usually at the end of a sentence or idea. Ideas, concepts, or sentences originated by other authors (literal citations) are cited within quotes (" "). Such statements are preceded or succeeded by a respective reference to the source. If longer passages are literally referred to, they are cited as standalone paragraphs that are indented. References using *cf.* (confer) mean that concepts are put in a dense form here, while the cited source contains more details. Interested readers should, therefore, consult the original sources for more information. Additionally, *cf.* is also used to reference to sections within this work, when concepts are discussed there in more detail.

- Words and phrases in *italics* indicate emphasis. Also proper names that may be confused with common English terms are italicised. While other works frequently use quotes (" ") instead, in this work, quotes are reserved solely for citations.

- This work includes a scale of figures and tables that were produced independently from any source. For all other illustrations, information on the source of figures and tables is given at the bottom right of the respective figure or table.

- For transparency reasons, *excerpts, quotes and phrases* from the data source (interviews) are cited within quotes (" ") as other references, and the words themselves are put in *italics* to distinguish them from other citations. As will be explained in the methods section (Section 3), the qualitative analysis is based on an in-depth interview. Accordingly, there is no need to differentiate between several interview sources.

- Non-essential information is given in footnotes to make the text more readable.
- Throughout the text, all headings (top-level headings as well as lower level headings) are referred to as *Sections* (e.g., Section 1, Section 1.1, Section 1.1.1).
- Meeting the gender-neutral requirement, this work tries to use the plural form whenever possible, since plural is gender-neutral in English language. In other instances, this work uses *him or her* when applicable, while keeping the readability of the text in mind.

2. Theory and reference frame

This section introduces the essential terms and definitions in the field of managing musical groups.

Musicians represent a subgroup of *artists*. However, it appears that term *artist* is often misused. Therefore, Section 2.1 initially gives a brief introduction to the terms *artist* and *artisan*. Then Section 2.2 defines the terms *band* and particularly *telephone band*, the construct that this research is dealing with.

Finally, this section closes with a discussion of music management and the role of *bandleaders as entrepreneurs* (Section 2.3).

2.1 Artists and artisans

UNESCO (1980) provides the most cited definition of *artist*:

> "'Artist' is taken to mean any person who creates or gives creative expression to, or recreates works of art, who considers his artistic creation to be an essential part of his life, who contributes in this way to the development of art and culture and who is or asks to be recognized as an artist, whether or not he is bound by any relations of employment or association."

Although widely referred to, this definition is both broad and vague. Accordingly, different studies use various ways to narrow down what is considered an artistic profession (e.g., Beckman, 2001; Dangel, Piorkowsky, & Stamm, 2006; European Institute for Comparative Cultural Research (ERICarts), 2006; Haak, 2005; Menger, 1999; Montag Stiftung Bildende Kunst Bonn, Akademie der bildenden Künste Wien, & Verlag für moderne Kunst, 2008; Schelepa, Wetzel, & Wohlfahrt, 2008; Throsby, 2007; Towse, 1996). As a result, it is rather inaccurate to compare these studies because statistics and other figures refer to different concepts of the artistic profession.

When we refer to artists, they make up a heterogeneous group of people that shows a large spectrum of professional and conceptual access to art (Menger, 1999). While in the early days the terms *artisan* and *artist* were used synonymously, each term has separate traits that have gradually emerged since the Renaissance and have been codified in encyclopaedias, treaties, and various institutions during the eighteenth century (Shiner, 2001, p. 15).

As can be seen form Table 1, although *artist* and *artisan* originally had the same meaning, the meaning of each term diverged at some point in history, creating two distinct constructs with accordingly different qualities emerged.

Table 1. From artist *and* artisan *as synonyms to the separation of qualities*

before the separation	after the separation	
artist/artisan	artist	artisan
talent or wit	genius	rule
Inspiration	inspiration/sensibility	calculation
facility (mind and body)	spontaneity (mind over body)	skill (body)
reproductive imagination	creative imagination	reproductive imagination
emulation (of past masters)	originality	imitation (of models)
imitation (nature)	creation	copying (nature)
service	freedom (play)	commerce (pay)

(Shiner, 2001, adapted)

According to this definition, an artist is a person who professes and practices an imaginative art.

Artists are creators from the point of view of imposing their (inner) vision to material or performance. Some examples of this definition are people who paint, draw, compose or have a particular talent for writing. Frequently, society views an artist as a creative genius in an ivory tower – a person who is detached from the world and who has sacrificed him or herself for the arts. However, this view does not take into account that artists approach life differently. There are two types of artists: artists who take economic realities into account and artists who reject these realities (Swedberg, 2006).

An artisan, in contrast, is a craftsperson. Artisans are skilled in their fields of expertise in an applied art; they apply their talents to reproduce others' imagination in the arts. The driving forces for artisans are commerce and receiving payment. Some examples of this definition include woodworkers, architects, and musicians who apply their instrumental or vocal skills to music (created by someone else) for commercial reasons rather than for self-expression.

Despite the clear separation of qualities described above, it appears that the term *artist* dominates public discussion, even when referring to artisans. Based on this ambiguous use of the terms, this work postulates that the two described characteristics of artist and artisan reflect the two extremes (archetypes) on a spectrum of characteristics (artist vs. artisan). Typically, individuals hold characteristics of both artists and artisans. The particular mix of these characteristics determines whether an individual is considered an artist or an artisan.

To make the definition of an artist more concrete, one well-accepted approach is to measure an individual or craft against the following eight factors (Frey & Pommerehne, 1989):

- amount of time spent on artistic work,
- amount of income derived from artistic activities,
- quality of artistic work produced,
- reputation as an artist among the general public,
- recognition among other artists,
- membership in a professional artists' association, and
- subjective self-evaluation of being an artist.

The creators of this approach themselves (Frey & Pommerehne, 1989) question whether this list is complete, balanced, and satisfies a particular study's needs. Plus, when it comes to practice, applying these criteria becomes rather difficult. Consequently, different studies use various methods to narrow down artistic professions. Due to the vast difficulty in defining the population of artists (Karttunen, 1998), existing studies have been based on differing definitions of the artistic profession, which makes it difficult to make comparisons among them.

For this work's purposes, we refer to musicians in their *role as artisans*, keeping in mind that artisans may also hold characteristic traits of artists (cf. Dudek, Bernèche, Bérubé, & Royer, 1991; Throsby, 2007).

2.2 The definition of a band

While a large scale of musicians perform solo (solo artist, solo musician), many artists form or join groups, ensembles, orchestras, etc. for at least a portion of their careers.

Ensembles and bands can be categorised in various ways. The next paragraphs are devoted to categorisations by size, genre, and method of assembly.

Categorisation of musical groups by size

A musical ensemble is a group of two or more musicians who perform music, either instrumental or vocal. A group of two musicians is called duo, three musicians a trio, four musicians a quartet, five musicians a quintet, and six musicians a sextet. Although names for higher numbers of musicians exist (e.g., septet, octet), these are rarely used. Individuals simply refer to larger groups of musicians as large bands, ensembles, choirs or orchestras.

A big band typically consists of approximately 12 to 25 musicians. While many terms are used to reference big bands (e.g., jazz band, stage band, jazz orchestra), *duodectet* or any terminology that refers to the size of an ensemble specifically are rarely used in relation to big bands.

Categorisation of musical groups by genre

In each musical style, different norms have developed for the size and composition of ensembles.

In classical music, some ensembles group together instruments from the same instrument family, such as string ensembles or wind ensembles. Typical sizes are trios and quartets. Alternatively other ensembles blend the sounds of different musical instrument families, such as the combination of piano, strings, and wind instruments.

Rock ensembles are usually called rock bands. They typically include e-guitars, keyboards (e.g., Hammond organ, synthesizer), and a rhythm section, made up of a bass guitar and a drum kit.

Jazz ensembles typically include one or several wind instruments (e.g., saxophone, trumpet, trombone) and a rhythm section, made up of a bass instrument (contrabass, bass guitar), one or two chordal instruments (e.g., guitar, piano), and drums. Vocal jazz ensembles also include a singer and usually sacrifice one or several wind players.

Big bands include a five-part saxophone section, a four-part trumpet section, a four-part trombone section, and a rhythm section, made up of a drum kit, a bass instrument (contrabass, bass guitar), guitar, and piano. Frequently, big bands play vocal music, which means that they include one or more singers. Sometimes, one player of each section is omitted; for example, in the rhythm section, it is frequently the guitar.

Categorisation of musical groups by their method of assembly

Besides a categorisation by size or genre, bands can also be distinguished by the method of assembly, meaning how the band was formed.

When musicians agree on occasion to form a band, this refers to an *organic band* (Engh, 2006, 2008). Frequently, two or three musicians take the initiative and search for the rest of the line-up.

A major label[1] typically initiates a *synthetic band* (casting band) (Engh, 2006; Stein, Engh, & Jakob, 2008). The target group (consumers), musical genre, musical style, and instrumental/vocal line-up are usually defined in advance, and the music managers search for appropriate musicians to serve these needs.

One band type where the method of assembly plays a large role is the – in musicians' jargon – *telephone band* (N. N., 2008; Seilinger, 2010b; Strunk, 2006). A *telephone band* does not have a fixed line-up; instead musicians are only called in for a specific performance (e.g., concert, ball, event, *gig*). Decades ago musicians were typically called via telephone to ask about their availability and negotiate contract details. Nowadays, the telephone has partly been replaced

---

1   To date, the four major labels are *Universal Music, Sony Music Entertainment, EMI,* and *Warner*.

by other means of communication such as e-mail. Still, the telephone is one of the main communication channels used. The *telephone band*'s name derives from this process. The greater the number of people to be included, the more complex the process of assembling the whole band becomes (Seilinger, 2010b). Managing a *telephone band* can be compared to the management of a virtual organisation. Details on this topic are discussed in Section 2.3.

Sometimes, a *telephone band* can be the beginning of an organic band. However, this is not necessarily the case and is certainly not the original intent of a *telephone band*.

2.3 Music management: The musician as one-person enterprise

In sheer numbers, the music market is dominated by what official statisticians describe as small or medium-size enterprises (SMEs) (Kubacki & Croft, 2005); frequently, artists are self-employed and act as one-person enterprises (Bundesministerium für Wirtschaft und Technologie, 2009; Council of Europe & European Institute for Comparative Cultural Research (ERICarts), 2010; Deutscher Bundestag, 2007; Schelepa, et al., 2008; Statistik Austria, 2007).

Like that of any self-employed person, an artist's success does not only depend on his or her (artistic) skill, talent, and effort but also on his or her ability to succeed in managerial and entrepreneurial functions (Menger, 2001; Weaver & Bowman, 2005). This includes new developments on a technical, managerial, and economic level (Menger, 2001).

While the fundamental concept of traditional marketing – meeting consumers' needs – does not typically apply in high arts (Colbert, 2003), in the market where artisans perform, it applies to a certain degree. A manager or bandleader "who does not subscribe to these notions will be unable to provide the entrepreneurship and leadership necessary to develop his or her organisation" (Colbert, 2003).

A large majority of (music) artists – and among them bandleaders – seem to lack management and commercial knowledge and skills (Eikhof & Haunschild, 2007; Menger, 1999). Inevitably though, every bandleader has to deal with economic or management issues (Eikhof & Haunschild, 2007; Menger, 1999). Consequently, an appropriate educational background in the field of management and commerce are key factors for success.

Still, artists develop such management and entrepreneurial skills to a large extent on the market (Menger, 2001) because – with the large exception of the United States (e.g., Moussetis & Ernst, 2004) and the United Kingdom (La Valle, O'Regan, & Jackson, 2000) – art curricula concentrate on artistic skills but fail or neglect to prepare students for the business tasks in their professional lives (for details cf. Bauer, et al., 2011).

2.4 The *telephone band* as a virtual organisation

Davidow and Malone (1992) were among the first authors who discussed the concept of virtual organisations. They developed the vision of dynamic networks of organisations, where suppliers and customers work together (Haas, 2007, p. 15). The ideas behind the term *virtual organisation* are though as numerous as the amount of books in the world. However, only few derive definitions from their ideas (Jansen & Simon, 2008, p. 13), and the concept of the virtual organisation does not follow a generally accepted definition (Haas, 2007, p. 16). Instead, it is common to describe a virtual organisation by a set of specific characteristics. Some commonly accepted characteristics are the following (cf. Haas, 2007, pp. 16-17; Jansen & Simon, 2008, pp. 15-16):

- Independency: Regardless of any joint activities that companies take, the participants in the virtual organisation remain legally and economically independent (Mertens, 1998).

- Focus on core competencies: Cooperating companies bring in their own set of skills and focus explicitly on their core competencies. Each partner delivers a specific service that no other partner could individually perform better. Accordingly, the resources and knowhow are pooled in order to form a *best-of-everything* organisation.

- Project orientation: Virtual organisations emerge only with a specific customer request. Tasks and activities are only performed together during the specified project. Accordingly, the organisation does not produce for an anonymous market. Instead, the products and services are typically individual or complex services that are not standardised or pre-produced.

- Temporariness: Virtual organisations are temporary networks. The cooperation takes place to exploit short-term market opportunities. This flexibility enables companies to react quickly to the current market requirements by co-operating on market demand and dissolving after the requirement is fulfilled.

- One face to the customer: There is only one contact point to customers, offering services of products. Typically the virtual organisation has a brand name or a focal company – also called a *broker* or *hub firm* (Child & Faulkner, 1998, pp. 119-120) – that acts in the name of the whole organisation. As long as the contact point ensures quality and liability, there is no need to know about the *internal* processes and the involved partners of the virtual organisation. The internal structure is not identifiable (*black box*) by external parties (Picot, Reichwald, & Wigand, 2003, p. 424).

- Low formalisation: In general, the virtual organisation refrains from hierarchical structures. The organisation dispenses with the institutionalisation of central management function for the administration of the virtual organisation. Instead, the cooperation between partners is characterised by self-organisation and equal rights for all partners. Furthermore, virtual organisations are supposed to act with minimal rules and contracts. Instead, mutual trust reduces opportunistic behaviour (cf. Köszegi, 2001).

- Application of ICT systems: Sophisticated ICT supports the inter-organisational communication and coordination processes. ICT is often considered as *enabler* or *driver* of virtual organisations. The main advantage of ICT support is seen in process acceleration through quick communication. However, communication costs may also be reduced (Wüthrich, Philipp, & Frentz, 1997).

- No office: A virtual organisation neither has a principal office nor factory buildings.

These characteristics also apply for *telephone bands*:

- Independency: The bandleader, musicians, vocalists and roadies[2] all are one-person enterprises that are legally and economically independent. Each of the participants strives for his or her own individual business goals. Accordingly, every one-person business also has to bear respective risks and assume liabilities. When agreeing to participate at a specific event, a one-person enterprise is liable to the focal company (the bandleader), who is the contact point to the customer and assumes liability to the event organiser. Simultaneously, the enterprise bears the risk of losing a *better-paid* job that is offered only after having agreed to the first offer.

- Focus on core competencies: The cooperating one-person enterprises only bring in their core competencies that are required for the *telephone band*. The required musical parts in a band are predetermined. It is not possible for two individuals to play the third trumpet as this part is reserved for one person. Neither would it be possible for a saxophone player, for instance, to be appointed to a trombone part. There are never more individuals included in a *telephone band* than necessary and sufficient.

- Project orientation: A *telephone band* is initiated by a specific customer request to perform at a particular event. The service offered, i.e. the performance, is always tailored to the specific requirements of the event. Furthermore, a band does not offer any products that could be pre-produced for an anonymous market.

- Temporariness: A *telephone band* only comes together for a single performance. In other words, the project has a predefined end. Although the same one-person enterprises might reunite for another event, this is not typically case. A telephone band forms only after a specific customer request. Then, the bandleader assembles the required musicians, vocalists, and roadies. Whether or not a one-person enterprise will participate again in the virtual organisation depends on a set of requirements, such as availability, mutual satisfaction with recent performances, and the current core competencies required for the event.

---

2   A roadie is a person who loads, unloads, and sets up equipment. He or she is engaged with organisational tasks and frequently performs errands for musicians on tour or at a performance respectively.

- One face to the customer: The face to the customer (i.e., the focal company) is the bandleader, who is frequently also considered the manager of the *telephone band*. With his or her name, the bandleader ensures quality and liability. The customer is neither interested in the internal organisation of the band nor is it significant to know which musicians, vocalists, or roadies will participate. Sometimes though, the inclusion of renowned vocalists or instrumentalists may be considered as a criterion for quality service. In such cases, the bandleader, as the face to the customer, guarantees the desired quality and assumes liability for it.

- Low formalisation: The bandleader acts as the face to the customer and coordinates between customer requests and the participants of the virtual organisation. The bandleader can, thus, be considered the manager of the band. Still, this is the only hierarchical level in the virtual organisation. All other partners have equal rights and duties. Still, there is some *musical hierarchy* in a band. For instance, a lead singer's role includes the determination of how to interpret a song or a first alto player determines the musical phrasing[3] for the saxophone section. These *musical hierarchies* are a part of the roles and core competencies of the participants in the band. Typically, the band's participants act with a minimum of rules, which are typically *not* documented in a written contract. Instead, mutual trust prevents opportunistic behaviour. For instance, as musicians want to maximise their own business benefits, they will strive to be included in another virtual organisation or another performance. This requires non-opportunistic behaviour in order to maintain a good reputation.

- Application of ICT systems: For communication and coordination purposes, a *telephone band* uses any kind of applicable communication system. Mobile phone, e-mail communication, Voice-over-Internet protocol (VoIP), and instant messaging are the most common ICT systems used.

- No own office: *Telephone bands* do not have their own business premises or offices. The only room required is a rehearsal room. Typically, such a room

---

3   Musical phrasing relates to how individual notes are shaped (expression) among a group of consecutive notes. It also includes how notes are weighted and shaped relative to one another.

is rented on an hourly basis or one of the one-person enterprises might own a rehearsal room that he or she can place at the band's disposal.

3. Methods

As the management of *telephone bands* has hardly been studied, this work aims at contributing a base of research. Based on the assumption that the efficient use of information and communication technologies is rare in managing bands and orchestras, the analysis and suggestions for improvements will particularly emphasise the integration of additional ICT elements.

Since this research is interdisciplinary in its core (business informatics, management science, social sciences, and cultural sciences), it makes use of its related disciplines' methodology. As the next sections illustrate, this research demands an interdisciplinary approach.

Section 3.1 discusses the research approach. First, it outlines the essential five research strategies available (Section 3.1.1). Then, Section 3.1.2 derives the case study strategy as the best applicable strategy for this work's research and outlines the study design in detail. This section also determines and discusses the methods for data collection (interview, observation) and interpretation (phenomenologist approach). These methodologies are methods primarily used in social sciences. Section 3.2 outlines the language definition selected for the visualisation of processes. This method is basically a business informatics method. The evaluation methods (Section 3.3) applied in this context are essentially strategic methods from the management science domain.

3.1 The research approach

This section outlines the approach taken in striving towards this work's research goals. The specific research questions are:

- How are the processes for a focal company in a virtual organisation shaped?
- How can these processes be methodically supported, particularly with the use of information and communication technologies?

First, Section 3.1.1 discusses the five essential research strategies from a pluralistic view. Then, Section 3.1.2 outlines the study design in detail.

3.1.1 The research strategy

The research strategy represents the way of collecting and analysing empirical evidence. Basically, there are five different research strategies for procuring data: experiments, surveys, archival analyses (e.g., economic study), history, and case studies. Each has its particular advantages and disadvantages (Yin, 1989, p. 15).

Formerly, the various research strategies were arrayed in a strictly hierarchical manner. Case studies were assumed to be appropriate for the exploratory phase of a research. Surveys and histories were attributed to the descriptive phase of research. And experiments were considered as the only approach that was qualified for explanatory investigations. Now, however, the scientific community regards this hierarchical view as incorrect and has adopted a pluralistic view.

This pluralistic view claims that each strategy can be used for all three purposes, whether exploratory, descriptive, or explanatory (Yin, 1989, pp. 15-16). Whether a research strategy is appropriate for a particular research is – according to this pluralistic view – not based on hierarchy but instead depends on three other conditions: the type of research question, the extent of control that a researcher has over behavioural events, and the degree of focus on contemporary verse historical events (Yin, 1989, pp. 16-20) (see Table 2).

Types of research questions

Basically, research questions are differentiated based on the interrogative pronoun: who, what, where, how, and why.

How and *why* questions have rather explanatory character. Hence, they will likely lead to case studies, histories, and experiments as research strategies. Such questions deal with interdependencies and developments, which need to be traced over a certain *period* of time (Yin, 1989, p. 18). For instance, if you want to investigate why common musical understanding in an orchestra does not occur under certain conditions, you could do a series of experiments.

Research questions focusing on *what* may be of two natures. The first type of *what* questions is exploratory (e.g., What are the ways in which a tune can be played well?). The second type of *what* questions actually represents a *how* ma-

ny or *how much* line of inquiry (e.g., What have been the outcomes from a particular managerial reorganisation?).

Table 2. *Relevant situations for different research strategies*

	form of research question	requires control over behavioural events?	focuses on contemporary events?
Experiment	what (explorative)	Yes	yes
	how		
	why		
Survey	who	No	yes
	what (explorative)		
	what (how many, how much)		
	where		
	how many		
	how much		
Archival analysis (e.g., economic study)	who	No	yes/no
	what (explorative)		
	what (how many, how much)		
	where		
	how many		
	how much		
History	what (explorative)	No	no
	how		
	why		
Case study	what (explorative)	No	yes
	how		
	why		

(Yin, 1989, p. 17, adapted)

The first type of *what* question calls for an explorative study. In principle, an exploratory study tries to develop hypotheses and propositions for further inquiry. In this case, any of the five research strategies can be adopted (e.g., exploratory survey, exploratory experiment, exploratory case study) (Yin, 1989, p. 17).

Similarly to *who* and *where* questions, the second type of *what* questions strives to identify or enumerate outcomes. Accordingly, such research endeavours are more likely to favour surveys or archival strategies than others. Survey and archival strategies are advantageous when the research endeavours to describe the incidence or prevalence of a phenomenon or when the investigation tries to predict certain outcomes (Yin, 1989, pp. 17-18).

Summarised, this means that, *how* and *why*, questions are likely to favour the adoption of case studies, experiments, or histories. *Who* and *where* questions favour surveys and archival studies. *What* questions may either be exploratory (in which case any of the five strategies could be used) or about the prevalence of a phenomenon (favouring surveys or the analysis of archival records) (Yin, 1989, p. 19).

Extent of control that a researcher has over behavioural events

As outlined above, *how* and *why* questions or *what* questions of explorative character favour the use of case studies, experiments, or histories. Which of these question types is most appropriate for research further depends on the extent of control that a researcher has over behavioural events.

Experimenters need full control over events. Therefore, experiments can only be carried out when researchers have the full power to manipulate behaviour directly, precisely, and systematically. However, as the methods overlap, experimental science also includes situations, in which the logic of experimental design is applied, even though the experimenter cannot manipulate behaviour (quasi-experimental situations) (Yin, 1989, p. 19).

When no relevant person is alive to report (even retrospectively) what occurred, the researchers have to rely on primary and secondary documents or physical artefacts as the main sources of evidence. Consequently, they have virtually no access to or control over the events under investigation. Here, histories are the preferred research strategy (Yin, 1989, p. 19).

Also, the case study strategy can be adopted, when the relevant behaviours cannot be manipulated. In contrast to examining moments in history though, this strategy is preferred in looking at contemporary events (Yin, 1989, p. 19).

In summation, when the researcher trying to answer *how*, *why*, or explorative *what* questions has full control over events, an experiment may be the appropriate research strategy. However, histories and case studies are preferred when there is virtually little or no control over behavioural events (Yin, 1989, p. 19).

Degree of focus on contemporary as opposed to historical events

As already mentioned above, histories and case studies overlap in many instances and rely basically on similar techniques. Their major differentiation lies in their focus on contemporary and historical events respectively. While histories rely on past events (e.g., primary and secondary documents, cultural and physical artefacts), case studies investigate contemporary events.[4] Despite the similarities, the case study's unique strength is its ability to deal with a full variety of evidence. While history deals with the *dead past*, the case study has two sources of evidence that cannot be included in the historian's repertoire: direct observation and systematic interviewing (Yin, 1989, p. 19).

As has been discussed above, some research questions have a clearly preferred strategy. In other situations, two strategies might be considered equally attractive since the strengths and weaknesses of these strategies overlap (e.g., how and why a certain president got elected). Basically, all the strategies should be considered in a given situation.

---

4   Note that contemporary events refer to current as well as recently accomplished activities, while historic events refer to events that can be studied by, for instance, historic documents or contemporary witnesses.

Furthermore, the various strategies are not mutually exclusive. This means that it is possible to use more than one strategy within a study (for instance, a survey within a case study) (Yin, 1989, p. 19).

3.1.2 The study design

Based on the considerations discussed in Section 3.1.1, this section outlines the selection of the research strategy and methodology for addressing this work's research questions: How are the processes for a focal company in a virtual organisation shaped? How can these processes be methodically supported, particularly with the use of information and communication technologies?

After discussing the research environment and setting, we can derive the appropriate research strategy on a more formal basis by following the guidelines presented in Section 3.1.1.

Based on the general presentation of research strategies and influencing factors (Table 2), the following Table 3 highlights those factors that apply for the study performed (coloured cells).

This work's research questions are *how questions*. Since the processes of managing *telephone bands* have not yet been documented, a contemporary set of events is investigated rather than historical documents and artefacts. As this research aims to model the processes of managing a band in their natural environment, control over behavioural events is restricted and would even counteract the targeted objectives.

Based on these considerations, the choice of an adequate research strategy is rather unambiguous, as the case study strategy appears to be the most appropriate option in this context. When *how questions* are being asked about a contemporary set of events and when the researcher does not have control over these events, the case study strategy has a distinct advantage (Yin, 1989, p. 19). Due to the constrained control over behavioural events, the possibilities of social experiments are limited in this context.

Interestingly, the case study is the second most applied method in business informatics (Figure 2).

Table 3. Selecting the research strategy

	form of research question	requires control over behavioural events?	focuses on contemporary events?
Experiment	what (explorative)	yes	yes
	how		
	why		
Survey	who	no	yes
	what (explorative)		
	what (how many, how much)		
	where		
	how many		
	how much		
Archival analysis (e.g., economic study)	who	no	yes/ no
	what (explorative)		
	what (how many, how much)		
	where		
	how many		
	how much		
History	what (explorative)	no	no
	how		
	why		
Case study	what (explorative)	no	yes
	how		
	why		

(Yin, 1989, p. 17, adapted)

Basically, the research profile of business informatics follows the constructivist paradigm and focuses on constructivist-qualitative methods (Wilde & Hess, 2007, p. 284). Information systems research, in contrast, follows the behaviouristic paradigm and focuses on quantitative-empirical methods.

When comparing the research profiles of information systems and business informatics, it becomes apparent that case studies' conceptual and formal-deductive analyses are the common denominator (Wilde & Hess, 2007, p. 285). As a result, the case study is characterised as the borderline between the constructivist paradigm (business informatics) and the behaviouristic paradigm (information systems).

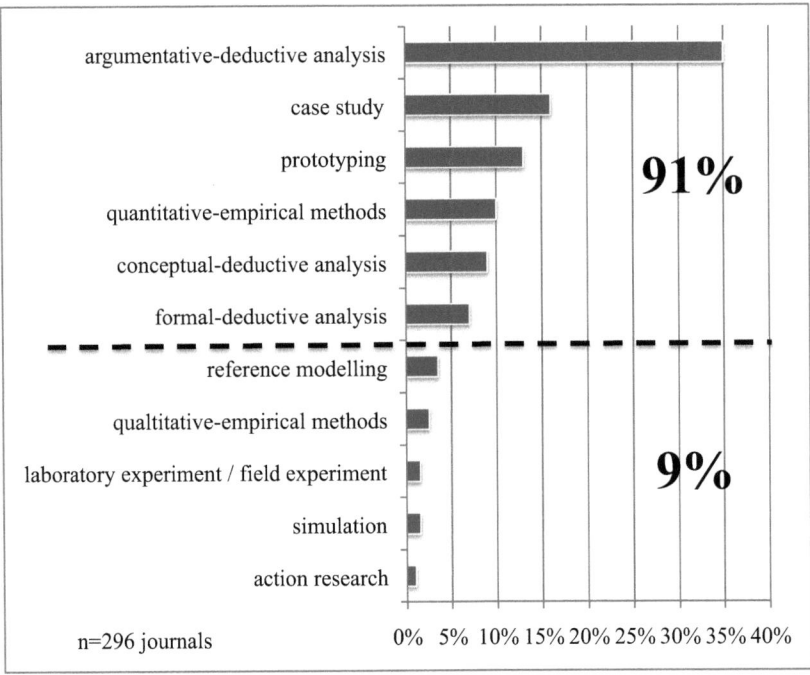

Figure 2. Frequency of research method use in the journal "Wirtschaftsinformatik" (business and information systems engineering)

(Wilde & Hess, 2007, p. 284, adapted)

3.1.2.1 The case study as a research strategy

Frequently, the term *case study* is not used in a clear and uniquely fixed sense (Hammersley & Gomm, 2000, p. 2). The following paragraphs will sketch the central components of its meaning and define this research strategy.

As Section 3.1.1 discussed, the term case study is frequently employed to identify a specific form of inquiry, which contrasts with the experiment and the (social) survey in a range of dimensions. An overview of these dimensions is given in Table 4. The case study differs from the social survey in two significant dimensions: the number of cases investigated and the amount of detailed information about each case. Typically, a case study refers to research that investigates a few cases in considerable depth. Surveys, in contrast, investigate a large number of cases while gathering only a relatively small amount of data from each case. Similar to the case study, the experiment also involves only a relatively small number of cases compared to survey work. However, what distinguishes it from a case study is the fact that it involves direct control of variables and behaviour (Hammersley & Gomm, 2000, pp. 2-3, 14-15).

Many authors regard a case study as not only a research strategy but also a research paradigm because it involves quite different assumptions about how the social world can and should be studied through underlying approaches. Then again, a case study is sometimes treated as a method to be used – when appropriate – like other methods depending on the problem under investigation. These oppositional views on case studies are formulated as the contrast between positivism, on the one hand, and naturalism, interpretivism, or constructivism, on the other (Hammersley & Gomm, 2000, pp. 3-5). This work follows the positivist view, considering the case study as a strategy.

According to the positivist view of case study, it is defined as "an empirical inquiry that:

- investigates a contemporary phenomenon within its real-life context; when
- the boundaries between phenomenon and context are not clearly evident; and in which
- multiple sources of evidence are used" (Yin, 1989, p. 23).

Table 4. A comparison of case study with experimental and survey approaches

points of comparison	experiment	case study	survey
number of cases	relatively small number	relatively small number (sometimes just one)	relatively large number
amount of information per case	small number of features for each case	large number of features for each case	small number of features for each case
setting	case is created in such a way as to control the important variables	naturally occurring case; in action research, study of cases created by the actions of the researcher but where the primary concern is not controlling variables to measure their effects	sample of naturally occurring cases, selected in such a way as to maximise the sample's representativeness in relation to some larger population
focus of interest	quantification of data is a priority	quantification is *not* a priority; indeed, qualitative data may be treated as superior data	quantification of data is a priority
goal of investigation	theoretical inference, development and testing of theory, or practical evaluation of an intervention	understanding the case studied in itself (with no interest in theoretical inference or empirical generalisation; however, there may also be attempts at one or other, or both, of these) alternatively, the wider relevance of the findings may be conceptualised in terms of the provision of vicarious experience, as a basis for naturalistic generalisation or transferability	empirical generalisation, from a sample to a finite populations this is seen as a platform for theoretical inference)

(Hammersley & Gomm, 2000, p. 4, adapted)

This definition points to the technically critical features of the case study strategy, which distinguishes it from other research strategies. The survey's ability to investigate the context is extremely limited. In using history and case study strategies, the phenomenon and context are inextricably interwoven. In contrast though, history usually researches historical events, while the experiment, by comparison, divorces a phenomenon from its context by controlling the context variables (Yin, 1989, p. 23). Briefly put, the case study could be the method of choice when the phenomenon under study is indistinguishable from its context (Yin, 1993, p. 3).

As depicted in Figure 3, case study research can be differentiated into two dimensions: single and multiple-case study designs. While a single-case study focuses on just one case, multiple-case studies include at least two cases, which replicate each other (either exact replications or predictably different replications) (Yin, 1993, p. 5). Furthermore, we can distinguish between a holistic approach with a single unit of analysis and an embedded approach where multiple units of analysis are used in a case (Figure 3).

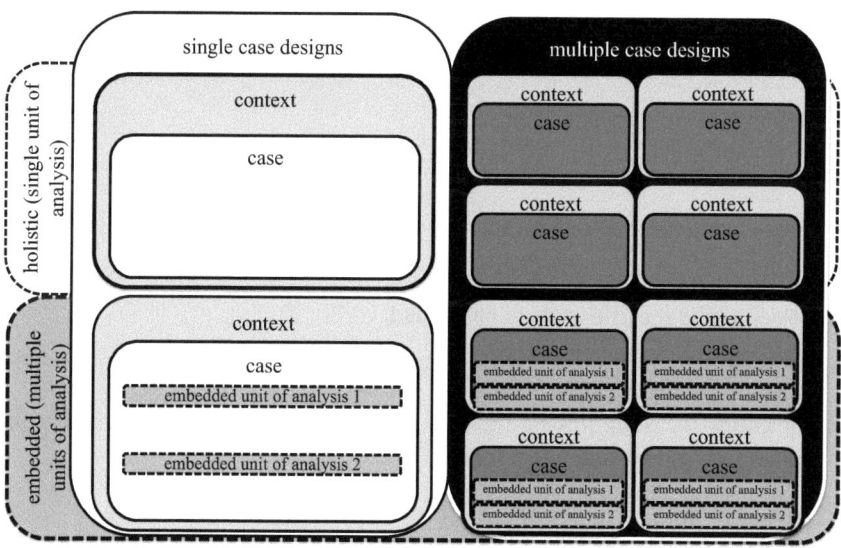

Figure 3. Case study research design

In evaluation research, case studies have their distinctive place. They are used (Yin, 1989, p. 23):

- to *explain* the causal links in real-life interventions (explanatory case study),
- to rigorously *describe* a phenomenon within its real-life context (descriptive case study),
- to *enhance* the evaluation by the intervention itself (again descriptive case study), and
- to *explore* situations in which the phenomenon being evaluated does not have a clear, single set of outcomes. Here, the case study aims at defining the research questions and hypotheses for a subsequent study (exploratory case study).

3.1.2.2 The case study design

Once the researcher has decided to use the case study, he or she has to go through following steps for specifying the case study design (cf. Yin, 1989, pp. 29-35; 1993, pp. 32-35):

- defining the research questions,
- outlining the propositions (if there are any),
- case study research design (identifying the major unit of analysis and deciding between single- and multiple-case study),
- selecting the specific cases to be studied,
- defining the relevant data collection strategies,
- indicating the logic linking the data to the propositions and determining the criteria for interpreting the findings.

Defining the research questions

Although the substance of research questions will vary across studies, the type of the question (who, what, where, how, and why) provides an important clue regarding the most appropriate research strategy to be used. The initial task for the research design is thus to clarify precisely the nature of the research questions (Yin, 1989, p. 23).

This first component of the research design – the research questions – has already been described in Section 3.1. Since this work attempts to answer how-questions (i.e. How are the processes for a focal company in a virtual organisation shaped? How can these processes be methodically supported, particularly with the use of information and communication technologies?), the research is explorative in nature.

Outlining the propositions

Theoretical foundation and related work need to be exposed in any kind of study. Case studies call for a deeper outlining of the investigation's underlying propositions, as they shed light on where to look for relevant evidence. Only studies of explorative character have legitimate reasons for not having any propositions. Still, every exploration should have some purpose. Accordingly, the design for exploratory studies should in any case state this purpose as well as the criteria by which an exploration will be considered successful (Yin, 1989, p. 23).

The propositions for this work have already been outlined in Section 1 and Section 2.

Case study research design

The third component of the research design is to define what the case actually is. While simple designs have single units of analysis, more complex designs may have multiple units, which may be embedded within each other. In the classic case study, an individual person (e.g., a clinical patient or an artist) serves as the case being studied. Typically, in such situations, the individual is the primary unit of analysis. If the study is performed as a multiple-case study, information about several relevant individuals (cases) is then collected and included in the study. In other research designs, the case might be a particular event or entity that is less well defined than a single person and may include multiple units, which are embedded within each other (e.g., a band may be the main single case, but the artists in this band might be an embedded unit of analysis). Frequently, it is difficult to define the exact borderlines of a case. For instance, if the unit of analysis is a group, the persons to be included in the group have to be clearly distinguished from those that are excluded in context of the specific case study. For almost any topic, it is necessary to define the specific beginning and end of the case to define the timeline (Merriam, 1988, pp. 44-47; Yin, 1989, pp. 31-33; 1993, pp. 32-33).

A case study can serve exploratory, descriptive, or causal purposes. If multiple cases are subject of study, they should follow a replication rather than a sampling logic. A sampling logic would indicate that the cases are data points representing a larger population. This is, though, an inappropriate rationale for case studies since the results of a case study cannot be generalised to an entire population; they can though be generalised to some theory, meaning that the results of a case study may or may not support a certain theory or may even be the basis for establishing a new theory. If the sampling logic is important to a research, other research strategies – such as surveys or experiments – are more likely to satisfy the investigation's needs than a case study would do (Yin, 1993, pp. 33-34).

Considering the explorative and simultaneously descriptive character of this research, it appears appropriate to follow a holistic approach with a single case study.

Selection of the specific case to be studied

The selection criteria may include significance (e.g., a particular case may be a critical case for the research it is embedded in), topical relevance (e.g., a particular case may be most suitable for the phenomenon being studied), or feasibility and access (e.g., a particular person or group is willing be the subject of the case study). Whatever the criteria, the case selection process may require researchers to collect preliminary information from a large group of potential entities and to perform a screening analysis in order to determine the cases actually included in the study (Stake, 1995, pp. 4-7; Yin, 1993, p. 34).

In accordance with the chosen case study research design, a *telephone band* is chosen as the major case, namely the *Vienna Ballroom Orchestra (VBO)* under the direction of *Gerald Seilinger* (Seilinger, 2010a; VBO, 2010).

This case is particularly suitable for this research for following reasons:

- VBO represents a virtual organisation with Gerald Seilinger acting as the focal company.
- It is a big band with the ability to add a strings section, resulting in numerous (i.e., 35) individuals to be coordinated (Seilinger, 2010b).
- The band targets large-scale events, such as the BonbonBall in Vienna (BonbonBall, 2010), which requires several months of preparation (Seilinger, 2010b), making the problem sufficiently complex to be modelled from a scientific perspective.
- The author of this work has been involved in management issues of this band, which gives the researcher the appropriate context (which is mandated by qualitative research methodology).

Definition of relevant data collection strategies

Unlike experiments or surveys, the case study does not claim any particular method for data collection: any method – from testing to interviewing – can be used for data gathering (Merriam, 1988, p. 10). In contrast to other research strategies, there is no particular moment when data collection begins. Essentially, data gathering begins even before there is any commitment to do the study because researchers bring their own background knowledge and may also be familiar with other (similar) cases (Stake, 1995, p. 49). Once researchers have decided to perform a study though, they have to choose from different kinds of data gathering strategies.

When the researchers decide for a one-time data collection effort, they typically dedicate a small number of days for every case to be studied. Much of the critical information is collected through interviews and documents (post-hoc data collection). The researchers may also decide to dedicate a longer period of time for data collection. Frequently, they spend a longer time period on-site for direct observation, which is also this model's advantage. However, it is more costly and requires access to the on-site facilities. Furthermore, the researcher cannot ensure that the relevant events will occur in the observed setting. And if they do occur, there is still the risk that the researcher not be at the right place at the right time to observe them (Yin, 1993, p. 35).

Despite these considerations, case studies have multiple sources for evidence, including documents, archival records, interviews, direct observations (with the researcher as observer), participant-observations (with the researcher simultaneously as a participant and an observer), and physical or cultural artefacts.

The principle of case study research is to incorporate at least *two* sources of evidence into the investigation, which will increase the study's quality substantially (Yin, 1989, p. 23).

Due to the explorative character of this study, qualitative research methods appear to be most appropriate.

Taking a phenomenologist perspective (Hycner, 1985), the only legitimate source of data is "the views and experiences of the participants themselves" (Goulding, 2005), which is taken as *fact*. Accordingly, participants are selected only if they have experienced the phenomenon under study (Goulding, 2005).

Serving this requirement in combination to the paradigm to incorporate multiple data sources, data will be collected from an *interview, direct observation,* and *participant-observation*.

As the bandleader of the Vienna Ballroom Orchestra (VBO, 2010), Gerald Seilinger (Seilinger, 2010a) could be identified as the main source of knowledge for the case, so data will be collected in a semi-structured interview, which will be recorded to allow for a thorough analysis (Flick, Kardorff, Keupp, Rosenstiel, & Wolff, 1995; Helfferich, 2005). Prepared questions serve as checklist (Miles & Huberman, 1994, pp. 105-110) in the data collection phase. Accordingly, the semi-structured type of an interview is selected because while structured questions serve as a general guideline, it still provides the interviewer with the freedom to react to the interviewee's answers with additional questions. The interview serves to gather as much information as possible, allowing the interviewer to structure the material.

As a second source of evidence, the researcher participates in parts of the planning and operation of the event in conjunction with the bandleader. These direct observations (Angrosino, 2009) are used to interpret the bandleader's explanations.

As a third source of evidence, the researcher can also further back-up on her observations on operational activities with her experiences as a roadie at the BonbonBall for several years. This participant-observation (Jorgensen, 1999) allows for a better understanding of the interviewee's explanations. It also provides the basis for the qualitative analysis of the data provided in the interview.

Furthermore, a follow-up conversation with the interviewee is used for clarification and fine-tuning of the gathered information.

The in-depth interview was held on 13 November 2010 and had a total length of 1 hour 14 minutes 3 seconds. The interview was literally transcribed with a total length of 10,915 words.[5]

The logic linking of data to propositions and criteria for interpreting the findings

For psychological experiments, it has been precisely defined how hypotheses and data have to be connected. For linking data to propositions, as needed in case studies, various methods exist. But none of these has become as precisely defined as methods for psychological experiments.

One promising approach for case studies is the idea of *pattern matching*, described by Donald Campbell (cf. Yin, 1989, pp. 109-113). This technique correlates several pieces of information within the same case with a particular theoretical proposition or assertion. For example, two or more potential patterns may be considered as rival propositions (e.g., an *effects proposition* and a *no effects proposition* regarding the impact of a treatment under study). Applying the pattern matching technique allows researcher to relate the data to the assertions, even in if the entire study consist of a single case (Yin, 1989, p. 23).

---

5   The interview was held in German. Qualitative quotes provided in this work are translations into English.

In many instances, it is not possible to use statistical tests to make comparisons, especially when undertaking a qualitative research. For instance, when applying the pattern matching technique, the challenge is to define how close a match has to be in order to be considered a match.

There is no precise methodology of qualifying the criteria for interpreting these types of data and findings. In fortunate cases, the different patterns will be sufficiently contrasting so that the findings can be interpreted in terms of comparing at least two rival propositions (Yin, 1989, p. 23).

The phenomenologist approach does not prescribe a strictly defined procedure (Hycner, 1985; Miles & Huberman, 1994). Still, Colaizzi (1978, cited by Goulding, 2005) suggests a series of seven steps that provide the researcher "with an understanding of the world that contributes towards the development of theory" (Goulding, 2005):

1.) In a first step, the researcher has to read the participants' narratives to acquire a feeling for their ideas. Only then, it is possible to understand them fully.
2.) The next step requires the researcher to identify keywords and sentences relating to the phenomenon under study (i.e., extracting significant statements).
3.) For each of the significant statements, the researcher has to formulate meanings.
4.) This process is iterated across participants' narratives for clustering meaningful themes. This step may require returning to the informants to validate interpretation.
5.) In a next step, the researcher integrates the resulting, clustered themes into a rich description of the phenomenon under study.
6.) Then the themes are reduced to an essential structure that explains the phenomenon.
7.) Finally, the researcher may return to the informants in order to crosscheck interpretation.

For the case study under investigation, these steps are operationalized as the following paragraphs describe.

First, the audio-recorded interview is transcribed. The transcription of the in-depth interview is read several times. Additionally, the researcher reflects on her own observations and takes notes. Similarly, these notes are read several times.

Then the text passages that refer to activities in managing the *telephone big band* are identified. The researcher reflects on the meanings of these activities and develops an understanding of their implications.

In a next step, the identified activities are clustered to themes. To allow for a thorough analysis of the contents, text is structured, and information is visualised in graphical models (Miles & Huberman, 1994). Displaying data in graphs is simultaneously an activity of data reduction in the data analysis process (Miles & Huberman, 1994, pp. 10-11). For this purpose, the activities are modelled using Unified Modeling Language (UML) for activity diagrams (Object Management Group, 2010b). In this phase of analysis though, the researcher does not (yet) adhere to all requirements of the modelling standard. Due to their complexity and autonomy, themes that include a range of activities are later modelled as sub-processes (for details on the visualisation language cf. Section 3.2).

With the help of the diagrams, the phenomenon is described verbally. For this purpose the transcriptions and notes are revisited to allow referencing direct quotes and phrases.

In a next step, both the diagrams and the descriptions are restructured and reduced to present the essential structure.

In a reflection phase, preliminary findings (models) are discussed with the interviewee and accordingly validated (Miles & Huberman, 1994). Results of the reflection are integrated in the final model.

Using a design science research approach (Hevner, March, Park, & Ram, 2004; van Aken, 2005), the final results are modelled adhering to using Unified Modeling Language (UML) for activity diagrams in the version 2.3 (Object Management Group, 2010b) and Entity Relationship Modeling (ERM) (Chen, 1976).

For deriving implications and suggestions for process improvement with particular view to ICT elements, a SWOT analysis (Hill & Westbrook, 1997; Weihrich, 1982) (cf. Section 3.3) is performed.

3.2 Language definition for the visualisation of processes

This work's objective is to describe and evaluate the process model of managing a *telephone big band*. Accordingly, we have to choose a method for process descriptions, which may describe processes graphically.

Literature suggests a multitude of description languages. Therefore, it is difficult to give a complete and disjunctive classification. Generally, on a broad level of granularity, we can distinguish (Leinenbach, 2000):

- semiformal languages for structuring,
- formal languages for specifying and preparing machine implementation, and
- machine-oriented programme languages for compilation.

The requirements of this work demand for a detailed understanding of the process models, which is fundamentally provided by semiformal description languages. Two widely used graphical standards in semiformal languages are Unified Modeling Language (UML) (Object Management Group, 2010b) – and UML activity diagrams specifically – as well as the Business Process Modeling Notation (BPMN) (Object Management Group, 2010a; White & Miers, 2008). Both languages are easy to understand by people with non-technical background (Ko, Lee, & Lee, 2009, p. 759). Basically, the main differences between BPMN and UML can be understood by considering the intended users of both notations. While UML is primarily targeted for software developers, BPMN was invented for business analysts (Ko, et al., 2009, p. 758). The UML 2.x developments though upgraded the activity diagram to accommodate business analysts as well (Ko, et al., 2009, p. 758).

Against this background, this work will apply the UML 2.3 standard (Object Management Group, 2010b) and UML activity diagrams in particular.

Activity diagrams are constructed from a limited repertoire of shapes, connected with arrows. Figure 4 illustrates the used constructs for process description with UML activity diagram notation according to UML Version 2.3 (Object Management Group, 2010a).

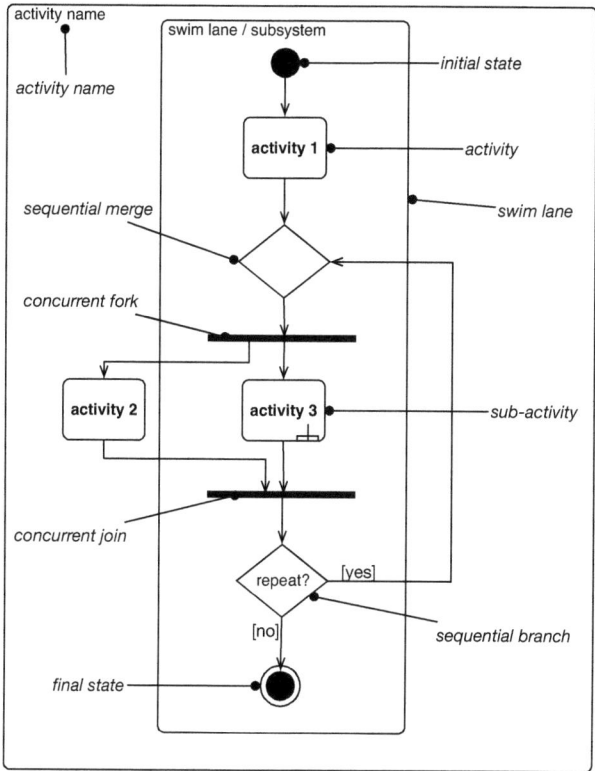

Figure 4. Quick reference for UML activity diagram notation according to UML 2.3

The most important shape types are:

- a black circle representing the start (initial state) of a workflow,
- an encircled black circle representing the end (final state),
- rounded rectangles representing activities,
- rounded rectangles with a rake at the right bottom representing sub-activities,
- diamonds with representing decisions,

- bars representing the start (concurrent fork) or end (concurrent join) of concurrent activities, and

- arrows connecting shapes representing the order in which activities happen.

Using solid vertical lines, the contents of an activity diagram may be organized into partitions (so-called swim lanes). Swim lanes do not have a formal semantic interpretation. In business process modelling, they are typically used to represent an organizational unit of some kind.

Arrows always run from the start (initial state) towards the end (final state). Hence, activity diagrams can be regarded as a form of flow charts.

3.3 Instruments of evaluation

This work aims to improve the processes involved in managing a *telephone big band*. In other words, considering the current situation and the targeted situation, we have to define a strategic plan for how to manage a *telephone big band*. Strategic planning is the process of defining a direction (strategy) for an organisation or business and making decisions on the allocation of resources to pursue this strategy. Resources include capital as well as people (Amason, 2010).

Various evaluation methods and tools can be used in strategic planning, including the most commonly used tools PEST analysis and SWOT analysis (Frost, 2003).

PEST is an acronym representing [P]olitical, [E]conomic, [S]ocio-cultural, and [T]echnological factors. Sometimes the PEST analysis is also called STEP analysis (cf. Clulow, 2005), the order of the initial letters being changed.

Basically, the PEST analysis (Peng & Nunes, 2007) looks at the external business environment (macro-environmental factors). It examines the impact of each of the four PEST factors on the business as well as their interplay with each other. The results of the analysis can be used to take advantage of the opportunities and to counteract threads by making contingency plans (Amason, 2010).

Also the SWOT analysis is a strategic planning method (cf. Hill & Westbrook, 1997; Weihrich, 1982). SWOT is an acronym representing [S]trength, [W]eaknesses, [O]pportunities, and [T]hreats (Figure 5). While SWOT is the most commonly referenced term, some authors (e.g., Weihrich, 1982) use the acronym TOWS, changing the order of the initial letters.

SWOT analysis considers both an internal as well as an external view. Subsequently, it is more flexible in its application than PEST, which is used to assess external factors only. SWOT analysis may be applied to any phase of business because it analyses the internal workings of a business' activities.

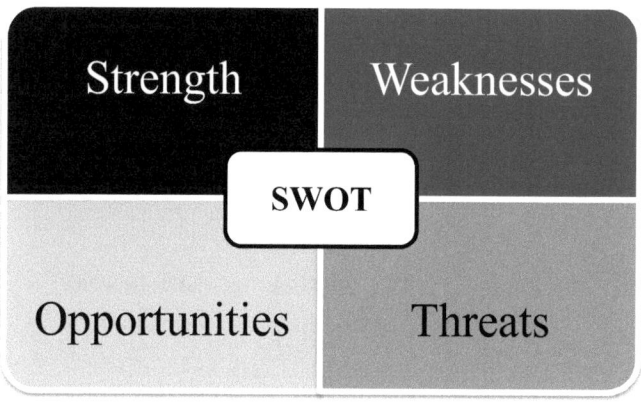

Figure 5. The four SWOT dimensions

Typically, the four dimensions of the SWOT analysis are visualised in a SWOT matrix (Figure 6) as introduced by Weihrich (1982). First, for each dimension a list is given. Based on these lists, respective strategies are derived, considering one internal and one external dimension at a time. Accordingly, we can derive four strategies: a SO strategy (strengths, opportunities), a WO strategy (weaknesses, opportunities), a ST strategy (strengths, threats), and a WT strategy (weaknesses, threats).

A market player would like to be in a position where he or she can maximise both, strengths and opportunities (SO strategy). The WO strategy attempts to minimise the weaknesses while maximising the opportunities. The ST strategy is based on the strengths, meaning it can deal with the external threats that a market player is facing. In general, the aim of the WT strategy is to minimise both weaknesses and threats. Indeed, a market player faced with external threats and having to cope with internal weaknesses may be in a precarious position, fighting for survival (cf. Weihrich, 1982, p. 61).

While strategic planning has a long history in the military, in the business world, predominantly product-orientated companies have extensively made use of it as early adopters (Weihrich, 1982, p. 66). Only later, this analysis' value was seen for service-oriented businesses (e.g., Andrews, 2009; Bernroider, 2002; Glaister & Falshaw, 1999; Stonehouse & Pemberton, 2002).

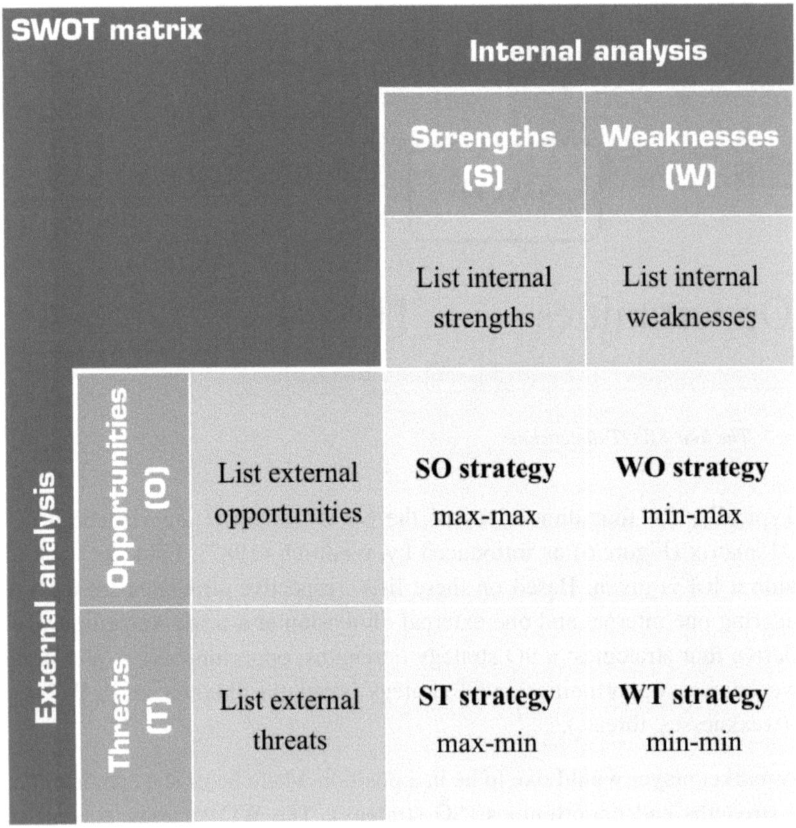

SWOT matrix		Internal analysis	
		Strengths (S)	**Weaknesses (W)**
		List internal strengths	List internal weaknesses
External analysis	Opportunities (O)	List external opportunities	**SO strategy** max-max	**WO strategy** min-max
	Threats (T)	List external threats	**ST strategy** max-min	**WT strategy** min-min

Figure 6. Matrix representation of the SWOT analysis

(Weihrich, 1982, p. 60, adapted)

Although some, Hill and Westbrook (1997) for instance, claim that the SWOT analysis is out-dated and strategic managers should take up newer and better approaches, more than a dozen years after this claim, this method is still widely used. This is probably due to the fact that the SWOT analysis is one of the most straightforward approaches for analysing the situational strategic position (Hill & Westbrook, 1997, p. 46).

Indeed, although literature on strategic issues in artist and music management is scarce, existing contributions predominantly make use of the SWOT analysis (e.g., Allen, 2007, pp. 146-148; Music Council of Australia (MCA), 2009; van Bree, 2009, pp. 33-36).

As this work pursues the improvement of the internal processes of the organisation, the SWOT analysis appears more applicable than the PEST analysis because the latter focuses on external factors. For improving internal processes, it is necessary to analyse internal factors that highly affect internal processes as well as external factors that may affect the internal processes.

Although the SWOT analysis is considered as an instrument for strategy development, this concept leaves it open to the applicant *how* strategies should be developed; and how these should be translated into concrete actions. Accordingly, researchers are required to explicate their specific approach. For the present work, we took following course of action:

In the first step of the analysis, the researcher evaluates the current situation. This evaluation is informed by the transcribed interview with the manager, the researcher's notes of direct observation, and the experience from participation-observation. Individual brainstorming was used to identify the pros and cons of the current situation.

Then, based on this analysis, appropriate strategies are derived. The mind mapping technique was used to identify overall ideas and strategies that could improve the situation. The researcher introduces a draft, which is discussed with the manager until both agree about the strategies in terms of need and feasibility. These strategies are then integrated in the SWOT matrix.

By restructuring and clustering the identified strategies, the researcher aggregates them to some overall strategies.

Considering these overall strategies, top-down brainstorming leads to the restructuring of the main process; particularly with respect to preponing planning activities to before the event (cf. Section 4.3). This creativity process is supported by the mind mapping technique.

On the level of sub-processes, we analyse for their fit with the overall strategies and introduce changes as needed. This requires considering each activity in the respective sub-process and analysing whether it is in line with the overall strategies (bottom-up approach). Here the focus lies on the deployment of electronic means and outsourcing. Again, a mind mapping technique is applied to collect innovative ideas.

Taking a bottom-up approach again, the modified sub-processes are then consolidated and integrated into the main process of performing at the event, adapting the sequencing of activities and sub-processes as needed.

4. Case study

As has been outlined in Section 3.1.2.2, the case under investigation is the Vienna Ballroom Orchestra (VBO) under direction of Gerald Seilinger (Seilinger, 2010a; VBO, 2010). Gerald Seilinger is not only the bandleader but can also be regarded as the *manager* of the band. He therefore acts as the focal company of the virtual organisation (i.e., VBO).

The VBO is a *telephone big band* with about 22 instrumental positions to be staffed. Additionally, there are five singers, each performing both as the lead singer and as a part of the choir. Furthermore, the big band can be enlarged by adding a string section of about seven people, and four roadies support the band (Seilinger, 2010b).

Gerald Seilinger (2010b) points out, "*They are all musicians that are real good artisans who master their instruments, can read music – who master their trades.*" In addition to that, "*One should get along well [...] One has to be able to communicate 'externally' what is not written on the sheet music – so to speak musically.*" As long as this musical understanding and ability to communicate with each other exists, the musicians of the band are exchangeable. Still, singers are not as easily exchangeable as, for instance, the third trumpet. Singers are in the forefront. "*Naturally, a singer represents a personality who is foregrounded as front person. If this is a well-known or outstanding person, one cannot simply say, someone else is coming. [...] It is easier to replace musicians.*"

Something specific to the VBO is that the band plays many arrangements that Gerald Seilinger made especially for the VBO. "*Many of the arrangements would not exist at all for big bands.*" A great proportion of big bands play arrangements sold on the market. The self-made arrangements are thus an asset to the VBO.

Despite its own arrangements, VBO is a big band that plays rather commercial music. "*One can incorporate artistic elements into the arrangements. That is possible. This is sophisticated commerce then. Let us call it that.*"

A big event, for which VBO is booked, is the yearly BonbonBall in Vienna at the Konzerthaus (BonbonBall, 2010). Here, Gerald Seilinger is not only responsible for the VBO but also takes over the organisation of the stages, including the music of two of the four dance halls (Seilinger, 2010b). "*The whole organisation of the stage is my responsibility. This means, when there is a star guest at midnight and before, and in-between something: [he wants to know] when it is his turn, when he has sound check, [I need] to communicate this,... Everything related to the two stages – in the Schubert hall and the Main hall – and concerns the music, touches my person.*"

Consequently, this part of the event management involves many people and numerous tasks, making the coordination of these tasks and people difficult. The following section (Section 4.1) describes the current situation of the involved processes. Section 4.2 analyses this situation by means of a SWOT analysis. Finally, Section 4.3 presents suggestions for improvements. It particularly considers ICT elements for process support.

4.1 Current situation – process model

Handling a telephone big band for the performance at the BonbonBall entails a complex organization process. Figure 7 illustrates the process from the project's kick off until the completion of all tasks.[6]

4.1.1 Initiation and pre-event planning

The process starts with an agreement with the event organiser. This is the kick off for the organisation of the *telephone band* VBO. The first task is dedicated to organising the musicians (Figure 8).

In a first step, the manager informs the approved cast via e-mail that VBO is booked again and asks whether they want to participate. This e-mail is only addressed to those musicians of the approved cast, people who the manager was satisfied with last time. Those musicians that do not answer the e-mail within a certain time frame are contacted via telephone. *"Musicians are all artistic souls. This requires a personal conversation, a personal invitation and so on. [...] The e-mail is the first information to reserve the date. [...] The personal call is then simply for... well... I mean, you do not just order jeans."*

---

6   This section is largely based on the interview held with Gerald Seilinger, the bandleader and manager of the Vienna Ballroom Orchestra (Seilinger, 2010b).

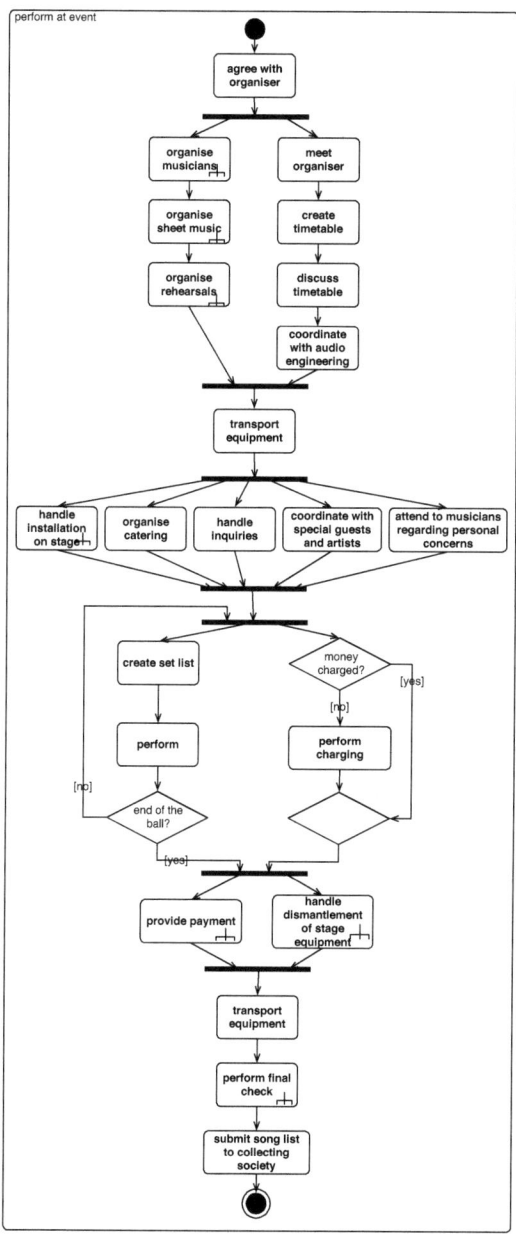

Figure 7. UML activity diagram for the performance at the event

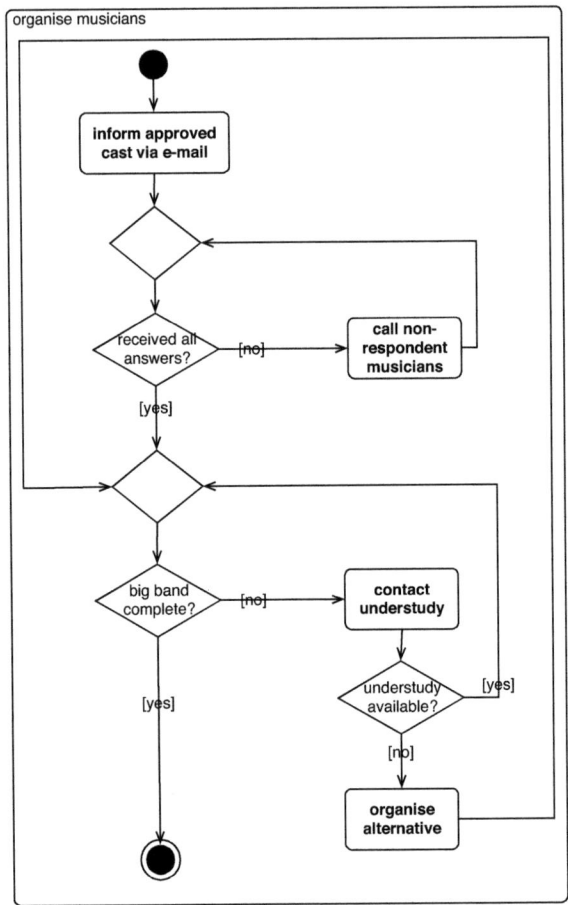

Figure 8. UML activity diagram for organising the musicians for VBO

If someone cannot participate (or does not want to or cannot be reached), the manager contacts the understudy. If neither musician is available, then the manager has to look for an alternative. "*I like to ask among the musicians. For example, if I need a drummer, then I ask the bass player because principally the bass player has to get along with the drummer in first place. [...] If those two cannot groove together, then it is already fatal. [...] If I am satisfied with the bass player and believe he plays well, then he probably has a drummer with whom I will be satisfied.*" These activities are iterated until the big band is finally complete.

The next step is a rather complex activity. Essentially it comprises of two tasks that may be carried out concurrently and one task that is carried out when the other two are completed (Figure 9).

The first task is to organise sheet music for the ball opening. As the dance master chooses the song for the opening, it is required to contact him and ask for the title and composer of the song. Then the manager looks for sheet music for this song in his own archive for big band. He contacts the leader of the string ensemble, which enlarges the big band, to see whether they have the song in their archive. If both the big band and the string ensemble have sheet music, the two bandleaders exchange sheet music and meet to compare and coordinate the strings and the big band arrangement. When it is necessary to adapt the arrangements – for example if the two arrangements do not fit together –, the manager adapts the arrangement for the strings section. If only the big band has sheet music and there is no sheet music for strings, the manager adapts the big band arrangement and includes parts for the string section. In any other case (i.e., when neither the big band nor the string ensemble has the sheet music or when only the string ensemble has it for the song), the next task is to see whether the song was already published for a big band (or published at all). If yes, the sheet music can be bought and then adapted, when necessary. If the song's sheet music is not available, the manager needs to create a new arrangement for the big band, including the strings section.

The second task, which can be performed concurrently to organising sheet music for the ball opening, is organising arrangements for new songs.

In a first step, the manager chooses new songs and checks whether the singers like the song, and if so, who will sing it and in which key. Predominantly using the Internet, he searches for suitable arrangements.

When the sheet music is available, the price decides whether or not it is bought. If the bought arrangement does not fit the requirements of the big band's instrumentation, it is adapted to fit. In any other case (i.e. either the sheet music is not available for the required instrumentation or it perceived as too expensive), the manager arranges the song himself.

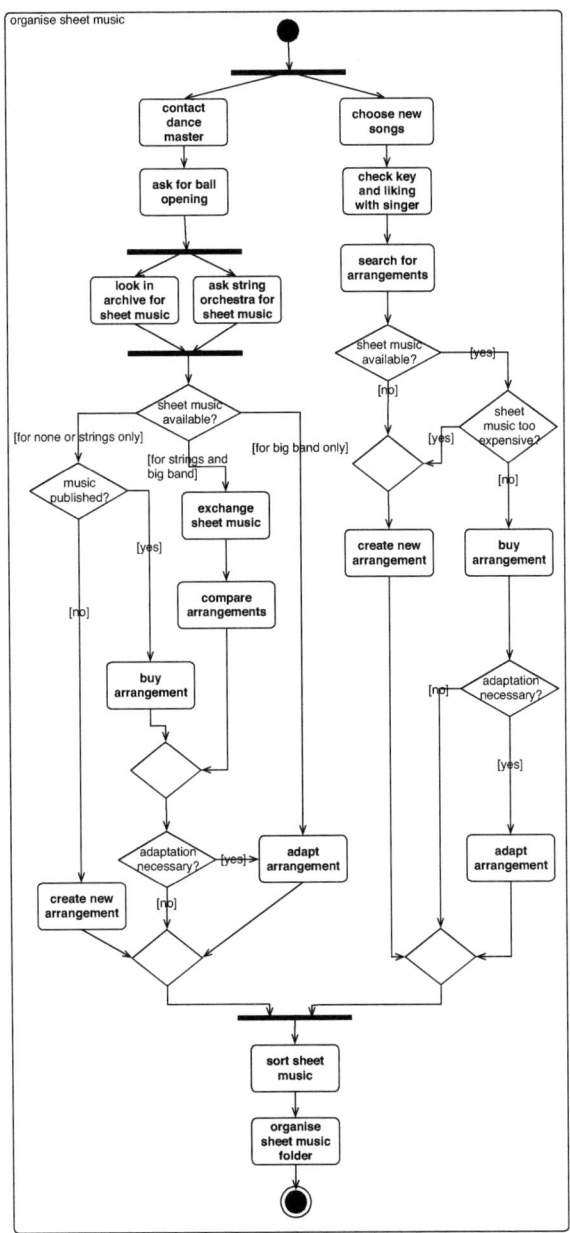

Figure 9. UML activity diagram for organising sheet music

When the sheet music for the new songs, including the one for the ball opening, is ready (either bought or arranged), the next task is to sort the sheet music into the sheet music folders. *"For each musician there is a separate sheet music folder. Those are 22 pieces. Parts for piano are always horrible because they are four, five, six, seven or eight-page. And one tends to underestimate it a bit, until you have made security copies... Per folder you then need four, five minutes to sort one piece of music [for one part]. Multiplied by 22. And this for, let's say, eight songs."*

Finally, after the sheet music is sorted, the next task is to organise the sheet music folder and put them into carrying cases to make them ready for transportation.

The next challenge in the overall process is to organise two rehearsals for the big band including the singers (Figure 10). *"Finding a joint rehearsal date for three musicians is already like hell. With five it is impossible, with seven it is a wonder."* Therefore, agreeing on two rehearsal dates for a 22-person big band with five singers is challenging and, in principle, impossible. *"Dividing the pay into paid rehearsals and performance pay could remedy the situation."*

For agreeing on possible rehearsal dates, the manager sets up a Doodle poll[7]. However, *"There are still some musicians who do not like to or cannot use the Internet. [...] Either they are not really Internet-literate. [...] Then there is a second category that simply do not feel like [using the Internet] anymore – thus, they do not use a computer at home."*

For this reason – and for those who do not reply in a timely manner – the manager calls the musicians that have not replied individually and inserts their answers into his personal list or directly into the Doodle poll. When the list of answers is finally complete, he chooses dates for the rehearsals. The first rehearsal is scheduled about two or three weeks before the event, the main goals being to reveal any major problems and try out the new arrangements. The second rehearsal is scheduled some days before the event so that the musicians have the rehearsal fresh in their minds for the event.

---

7   Doodle is a free, web-based tool that helps scheduling meetings and other appointments. For details see, www.doodle.com.

Finally, the manager informs all participants about the chosen dates via e-mail.

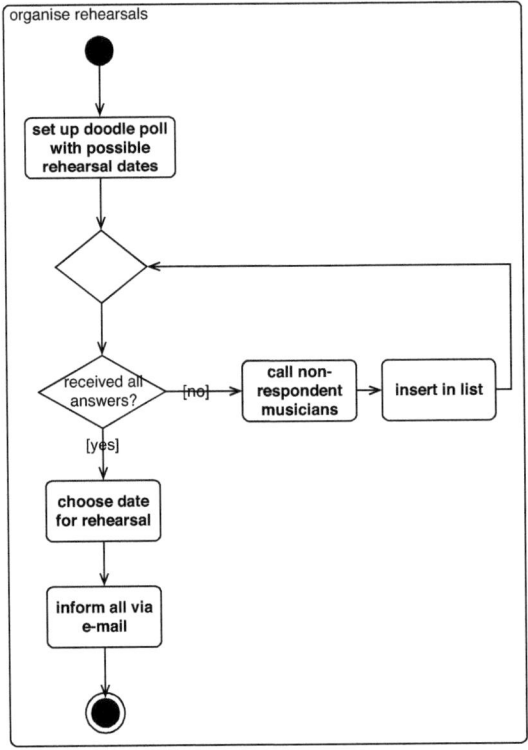

Figure 10. UML activity diagram for organising rehearsals

As can be seen from Figure 7 (page 49), some activities are carried out independently from the organisation of musicians, sheet music, and rehearsals. After the agreement with the organiser, it is necessary to meet with the organiser again to discuss the needs and special requests for the event as well as deviations from the previous year.

A very important task is the creation of the event's timetable. This includes scheduling the bands on stage in the Schubert hall and the Main hall. Additionally, the sound check and dress rehearsal of the dancers and sometimes also the special guests have to be scheduled for the day of the event. *"There are so many people involved. [...] And so you need to make a tight schedule so that this really works out well and nobody treads on each other's feet."* Because of its importance, a few weeks before the event, the timetable for the event is discussed with the organiser.

Another task that can only start when the timetable for the sound check is fixed, is the coordination with audio engineering. Audio engineering is provided by the location (i.e., the Viennese Konzerthaus). The coordination includes not only the communication of the timetable but also instructions for audio engineers with the requirements for the VBO.

4.1.2 Pre-event execution on the day of the event

The first activity on the day of the event is to transport the equipment to the Viennese Konzerthaus. Once there, different activities need to start concurrently.

One major task is the installation on stage (Figure 11). First the equipment has to be unloaded. On site, the music stands have to be organised. The staff on site already know the required number of stands. Still it is necessary to instruct people to bring them on stage and, if necessary, ask for more. Then the music stands have to be positioned according to the typical seating for a big band.

Once the music stands are positioned, the music stand lights can be organised in the same manner as the music stands; the staff on site already knows the required number of music stand lights, but they need to be instructed to bring them on stage. The music stand lights can be mounted on the music stands. It is then necessary to check, if all of them actually work. If not, the broken ones need to be replaced.

Similarly to the music stands, the seats have to be arranged according to the typical seating for a big band. Every musician needs a music stand and a chair – except the drummer who brings his own special chair.

After either the music stands or the seats are positioned, the sheet music folders are distributed to the respective seats or stands.

Simultaneously two recorders, which are part of the brought equipment, have to be organised. One of them has to be positioned next to the stage, so that it can record the band acoustically. The second recorder has to be taken to the sound engineers. They have to be asked whether they can take a live recording of the performance directly on the device. Further details on the recording need to be coordinated as necessary according the respective requirements on the day.

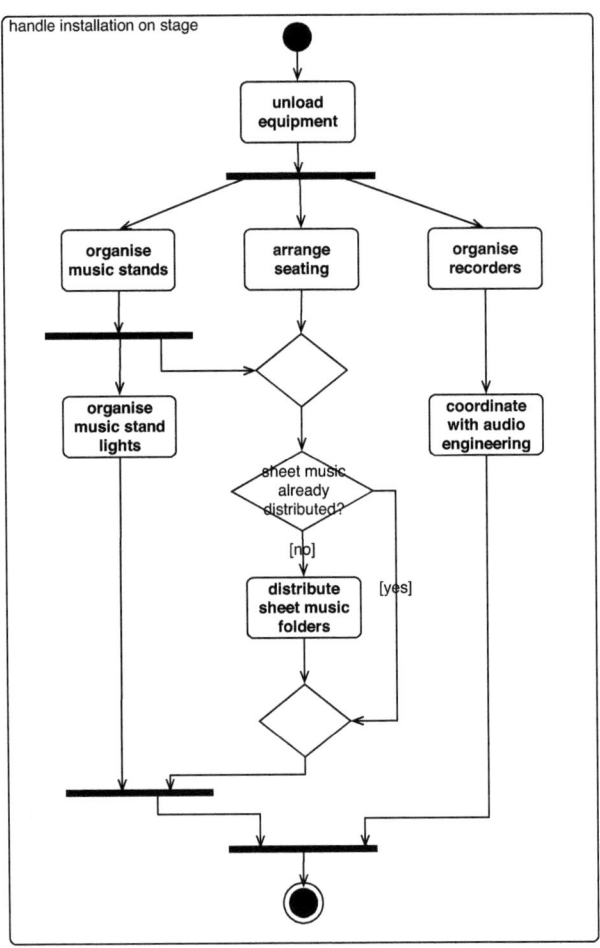

Figure 11. UML activity diagram for handling the installation on stage

In concert with the installation on stage, typically a number of inquiries need to be handled. *"Directly before the event, the phone rings constantly. [...] Everyone rehearses. Everyone wants to use the area. Everyone wants to know all at once how engineering works, when it is their time, how they can use the stage and so forth."*

At the same time – and also to prevent further inquiries – the manager coordinates with the special guests and further artists concerning rehearsals, sound check, and the final performance of the event.

Additionally, the catering for the musicians has to be organised with respect to timing, location, and amount. Although it is organised beforehand, it is important to double-check that the catering is indeed available when required.

Furthermore, the manager needs to address the musicians' personal concerns. *"They are all individual souls. Some are uncomplicated; some are very complicated. But you need to attend to all of them."*

4.1.3 Execution: performing at the event

Right before the ball's opening, the first set list has to be created (see Figure 7, page 49), which is subsequently performed. For each set that the band plays, these two activities are iterated until the event ends.

The set lists are organised in the band's breaks between performing the sets.

During one of the breaks, the bandleader must get the payment for the band from the organiser. Typically there is one break that is longer than the others. Accordingly it is the best choice to use that break for this transaction.

4.1.4 Post-event activities and closing

After the performance, it is time to pay the band and other associated individuals (Figure 12). Usually, individuals are required to bring a prepared fee note, which is a receipt for services rendered. Frequently though, people forget to bring their prepared fee notes. For these cases, the manager provides blank fee notes, which people can fill out at the event.

The fee note has to be checked for the value added tax (VAT) number, the signature, the date, and the correctness of the event statement. When the fee note is checked as correct, the compensation is paid.

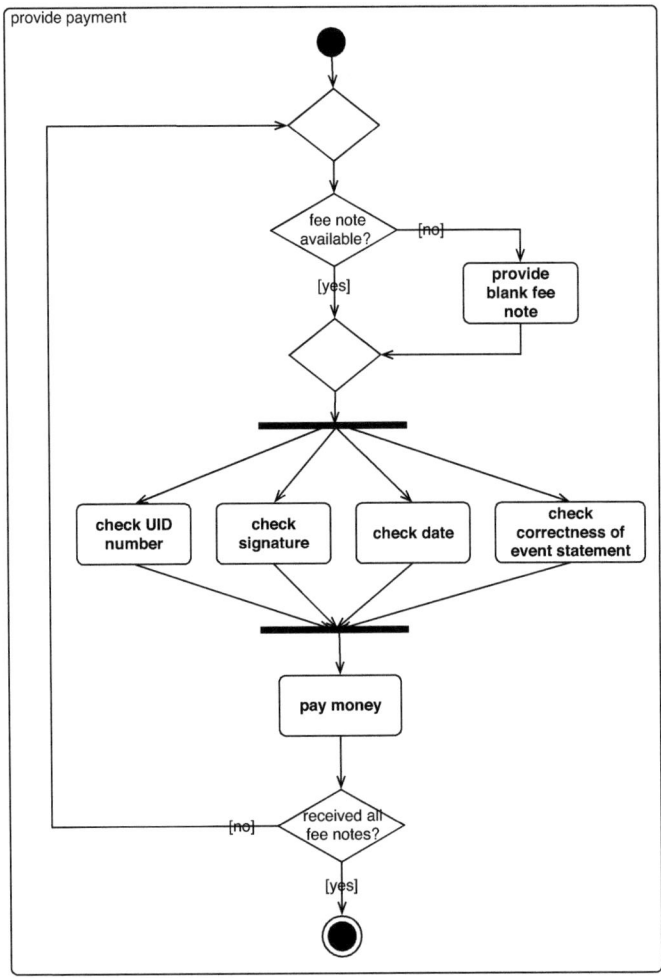

Figure 12. UML activity diagram for providing payment

Every participant (instrumentalist, singer, roadie) needs to fill out a fee note and have it checked by the manager.

At the same time, dismantling the stage equipment can begin (Figure 13). One task is to get the recorders – one from the stage, one from the audio engineers.

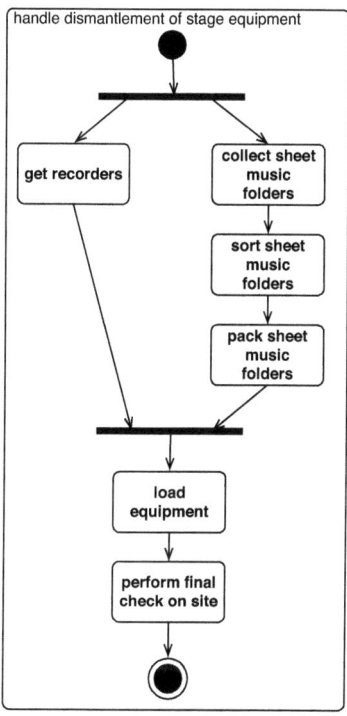

Figure 13. UML activity diagram for handling the dismantlement of stage equipment

The second task is to collect the sheet music folders and sort them by instrumental section (rhythm section, saxophones, trumpets, trombones). The sorted sheet music folders then must be packed into the respective carrying cases for transportation.

Next the equipment has to be loaded up. Before leaving the site, someone needs to perform a final check on site to make sure that nothing has been forgotten.

In a next step, the equipment can be transported back to the storage.

On the next day, the manager performs a final check (Figure 14). This final check comprises of three tasks. One of these is to check the sheet music to make sure that nothing has been forgotten on site. Second, all fee notes are checked again to make sure that everything is correct. Third, money is checked to make sure that payment calculation and compensation have been done correctly.

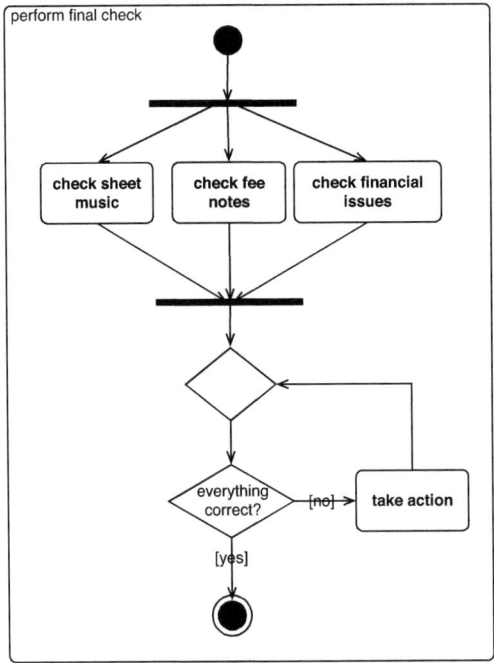

Figure 14. UML activity diagram for performing the final check

If everything is correct, the checking process is completed. If errors were detected, action has to be taken until everything is finally correct.

Finally, the process ends with submitting the song list to the collecting society. This can be done right after the event or any time later until January of the next year. After this, the entire process is completed.

4.2 SWOT analysis

This section analyses the organisation of the VBO using a SWOT analysis. In the first step of the analysis, the current situation is evaluated (Section 4.2.1). Then, based on this analysis, appropriate strategies are derived (Section 4.2.2). Table 5 depicts the SWOT matrix, including results of both sections.

4.2.1 Evaluation

The strength of the organisation lies in the detailed planning and consideration of diverse eventualities. For instance, the manager reports, "*I organise parking tickets because I know someone will definitely forget to take the parking ticket with him.*" He also organises batteries beforehand: "*Before the event fails [...] just because of a set of batteries, well – just to make sure.*"

The unique selling proposition (USP) is probably the fact that VBO presents new arrangements every year. Particularly, VBO has self-made arrangements that would not even exist for big bands elsewhere.

Furthermore, the manager has access to an extensive network of musicians. This makes it easy to find substitutes when needed. Asking a key person (someone with a key position in the band) to suggest an individual usually provides a good substitute. Typically such a person will recommend someone who will not only fit into the big band but who also plays in the way expected by the manager. Furthermore, because people will usually only suggest people that they like, the substitute tends to blend in well with the band on a personal level.

The prime weakness of the organisation is that the success of the band revolves around one person, the manager. In peak moments, there are more inquiries and tasks than he could handle simultaneously.

Table 5. SWOT matrix for the event organisation

SWOT matrix			Internal analysis	
			Strengths (S)	Weaknesses (W)
			<ul><li>detailed planning</li><li>new arrangements are unique selling proposition (USP)</li><li>good network of musicians available with an abundance of substitute musicians when required</li></ul>	<ul><li>centralised organisation</li><li>the manager is given too many roles</li><li>reluctance to outsource activities</li><li>almost no use of electronic support</li><li>self-imposed burden to present new arrangements</li></ul>
External analysis	Opportunities (O)	<ul><li>outsourcing of activities</li><li>well-elaborated, detailed preparation before the event</li></ul>	SO strategy <ul><li>complete and thorough planning with all eventualities before the event</li><li>use of network to find persons to outsource tasks</li></ul>	WO strategy <ul><li>giving the roadies more responsibilities</li><li>use of electronic means to handle organisational tasks before the event</li></ul>
	Threats (T)	<ul><li>work overload of the central person</li><li>when the manager is not available, the whole performance fails</li></ul>	ST strategy <ul><li>use of network to find persons to outsource tasks</li><li>thorough planning of all eventualities before the event</li></ul>	WT strategy <ul><li>giving the roadies more responsibilities</li><li>use electronic means to handle organisational tasks</li><li>limitation of the extent of new arrangements</li></ul>

Closely related to this difficulty is the fact that the manager is given too many roles. In projects, one person frequently takes on several roles. And in one-person businesses, it is one person who handles everything. Still, for an undertaking the size of the VBO, a division of labour could be advantageous.

Still, further analysis reveals that there is an underlying reluctance to outsource activities. *"One can outsource everything. Or a lot. But it is a question of having someone who you can trust is doing everything right. [...] However, it is more difficult to find someone trustworthy, who is well versed [in the field]."*

Furthermore, except for the Doodle poll and e-mails, new technologies are not used to support the complex processes. It appears that some behaviours such as telephoning 22 people personally, is now considered unusual and out-dated for assembling a band.

Additionally, the process of choosing new songs, buying or creating arrangements for big band, and sorting those arrangements into the sheet music folders is a time-consuming process. Furthermore, the organiser of the event does not even demand new songs. The manager self-imposes this challenge each year. *"Simply because one challenges oneself over and over again to offer something new, try something new."*[8] Having a big repertoire is definitely an asset for a band. Still, augmenting the repertoire complicates the process in the preparation phase of the event. From the viewpoint of process optimisation, it is thus a weakness.

A great opportunity for VBO would be to outsource the activities to people other than the manager. Due to the detailed planning, tasks could be assigned to, for instance, the roadies. This would take the overload of tasks away from the manager.

Another opportunity to create a better managerial process is to shift all the tasks and sub-tasks that can be handled before the event to the preparation phase. In doing so, the tremendous number of tasks that need to be performed simultaneously can be diluted.

---

8   Gerald Seilinger (Seilinger, 2010b) reports that arranging one song for big band for the event takes him on average four days.

A threat of the current situation is the work overload of the manager, who is the central person. Both in the preparation phase as well as during the event, he takes on many roles simultaneously and has to act and react on inquiries that relate to each role. This is a stressful situation for the manager, which can overwhelm him and ultimately negatively affect the performance. Additionally, those who have inquiries may not get the full attention of the manager, which can subsequently result in unsatisfactory answers. In the worst-case scenario, the musicians, the organiser, and the audience would be dissatisfied because inquiries were not handled as well as desired.

The fact that the entire process depends on one person poses a secondary threat. Consequently, if the manager is not available (for whatever reason), the performance – and with it the entire event – would fail.

4.2.2 Strategy development

This SWOT analysis (Section 4.2.1) induces particular strategies based on the combinations of strengths and opportunities (SO strategy), weaknesses and opportunities (WO strategy), strengths and threats (ST strategy), as well as weaknesses and threats (WT strategy). The following paragraphs are dedicated to these strategies.

The SO strategy would include a thorough planning with all eventualities, completed before the event. The network of musicians can be used to find well-versed persons to outsource some tasks to.

The WO strategy could include giving the roadies additional responsibilities and tasks. During the event's performance, the roadies are rarely required. Consequently, they could be deployed to perform diverse activities during the event. Furthermore, an increased use of ICT to handle organisational tasks could enhance the process performance.

The ST strategy suggests, similar to the SO strategy, using the network of musicians to dilute the manager's workload. Furthermore, the ST strategy would foresee a thorough planning with all eventualities before the event. This would particularly include an alternative plan on how to act if the manager were not available.

The WT strategy could, in accordance with the WO strategy, give roadies additional responsibilities to dilute the workload of the manager. Furthermore, the increased use of electronic means could also relieve some of the workload because some tasks would be easier or could even be automated. Finally, the WT strategy suggests limiting the extent of new arrangements. Choosing, buying, adapting, or creating such arrangements is very time-consuming. It is not required for a successful performance at the event, especially because the organiser of the event does not ask for new songs.

4.3 Suggestions for improvements with particular consideration to information and communication technologies

Considering the SWOT analysis and the derived, possible strategies (Section 4.2), this section focuses on process improvements that are easy to implement in terms of feasibility. From the perspective of business informatics, the improvements focus the deployment of new technologies and, more specifically, ICT elements.

From the SO, WO, ST and WT strategies, we can derive the following three strategies on a common denominator:

- elaborating a complete and thorough planning with all eventualities before the event,
- outsourcing tasks and activities, and
- using electronic means to handle organisational tasks.

Figure 15 illustrates the improved process for performing at the event. Activities that are carried out by someone other than the manager are accentuated in grey.

Because the main process (Figure 15) of the performance at the event is restructured and new activities are added, changes of sub-activities are necessary. Some sub-activities can be improved by deploying technology.

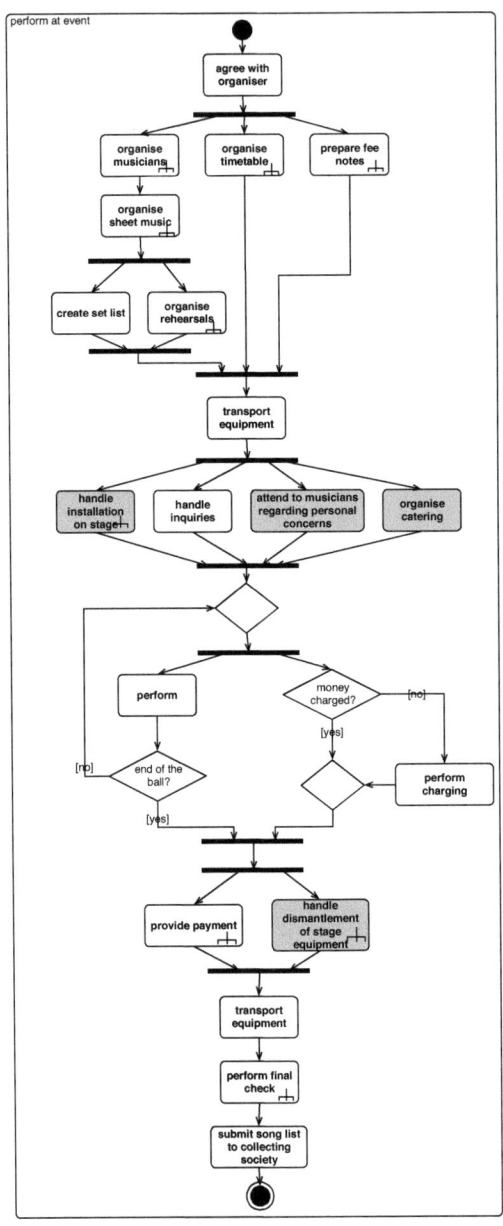

Figure 15. UML activity diagram for the improved process of performing at the event

The next paragraphs outline the changes of the main process. The following subsections discuss changes of sub-activities in detail.

To the manager, the day of the event is a very stressful time. Not only does he have to organise the transportation as well as the installation of the equipment on stage before he can perform with the band but he also is smothered with organisational tasks, including organising the catering, coordinating with special guests and artists, handling inquiries, and creating the set lists for each set that the band performs. However, some of the tasks could be done in the preparation phase before the event.

For instance, the set lists could be prepared in advance. Slight changes could always be made *on the fly* during the performance as a response to the audience. "*I already have experience so I know approximately how to make up the program, and I know what will work beforehand. However, if I recognise that, for instance, the slow waltz is not appealing anymore or the dance floor gets empty, then I would drop the next slow waltz and play a quicker tune.*" Accordingly, there is no need to create the set lists in the stressful short breaks between the performances because lists can be prepared in advance and minor changes can be handled during performance.

Also, the coordination with special guests and artists could be done in the preparation phase before the event. In this case, the manager would require the contact details of the special guests and artists (or respectively of their agents) before the event. In the current situation, the contact details are exchanged on the day of performance.

If the timetable is created at least a few days before the day of the event, it would be feasible to coordinate the appearances of the special guests and artists on stage as well as their dress rehearsals and sound checks beforehand. It is only necessary to inform them a few days in advance, for instance, by sending out the timetable via e-mail.

Without this beforehand information, the artists, special guests, or their agents must directly approach the manager before the event (while he is handling the installation on stage, organising the catering, attending to the musicians' personal concerns, or handling other inquiries).

Naturally, it is difficult to prevent some inquiries concerning the timetable. For this purpose, it would be beneficial to have the timetable displayed on screens or hung around the stage and backstage. If there are still inquiries concerning the timetable, people could be referred to these notices.

Furthermore, some of the tasks, which have to be carried out on site and cannot be efficiently supported electronically, can be outsourced to the roadies. For instance, attending to musicians' personal concerns can be delegated to one of the roadies. In this case, the musicians will not be attended by the *boss* personally, but they get one person that is (almost) fully dedicated to their individual concerns, which should be perceived as honour and acceptable alternative.

This person who is in charge of the musicians could also organise the catering, since this is a task related to the musicians comfort. This would, again, free the manager from some of the workload.

Plus, installing and dismantling the stage equipment could be entirely delegated to the roadies. They will be able to perform these tasks on their own, when they (1) have sufficient experience, (2) are well trained in doing so or (3) have a well elaborated instructional plan available at hand.

Additionally, the process of providing payment can be improved. This requires a preparation of the fee notes before the event. Details are discussed later in Section 4.3.7.

4.3.1 Organising the timetable

As already mentioned above, the organisation of the timetable requires a process change (Figure 16). Meeting the organiser and creating the timetable remain the same as in the original process. Then the process splits into two activities. On the one hand, the timetable is discussed with the organiser. On the other hand, a new activity is added: getting the contact information of the involved people. The organiser has all contact information and can hand it out. The timetable can then be sent to all involved people already before the event. If the organiser is reluctant to hand out the contact information due to privacy concerns, he or she could send out the timetable to the respective participants. In the latter approach, the organiser abides by the law because he or she does *not* hand out private information to a third party.

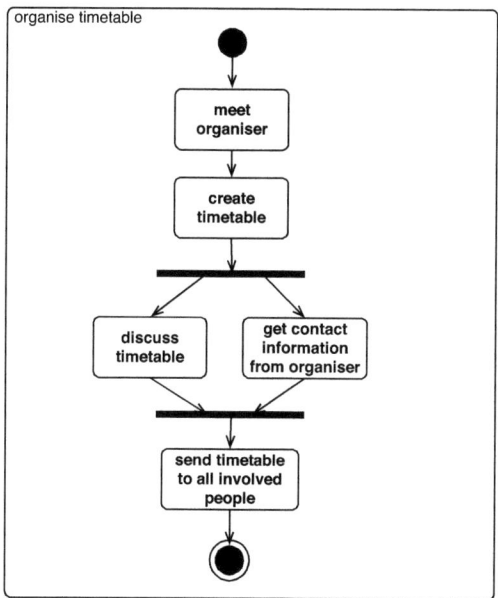

Figure 16. UML activity diagram for organising the timetable

Sending out the timetable to everyone involved makes everyone aware of the schedule. By receiving the complete list, they understand that there are a number of groups and people involved and that the schedule is tight. This can also reduce the number of delays that typically occur from latecomers.

The roadies must be informed of the timetable as well. Only then can they give appropriate answers to inquiries and free the manager from this task. As the timetable should be spread around the stage and the backstage area via displays or printed out posters, the roadies should naturally be well informed.

4.3.2 Installing and dismantling stage equipment

Installing and dismantling stage equipment should also include posting or displaying the timetable or removing the information respectively.

Furthermore, the provision of checklists and detailed written (or symbolised) instruction would also enable roadies without prior experience to handle the job correctly and efficiently. Such an instruction sheet should include a graph of the seating arrangement (stage plan), clear information on where to get the music stands and music stand lights, and detailed instruction on where to position the recorders.

It might be time consuming to make concise and clear instructions. However, this is a one-time investment because such instructions could be reused every year with even the possibility of use for performances at other venues (Figure 17 and Figure 18).

For communication among the roadies, a push-to-talk (PTT) or push-to-talk over cellular (PoC) system seems useful.

PTT is a method for half-duplex communications, using a momentary button to switch from voice reception to voice transmission mode. In other words, one person speaks, the others receive. PTT has its roots in military radios and is also broadly used in private networks, such as coastal naval radio for leisure boating. PoC is a service option for a cellular phone network. The main difference between PTT and PoC systems is that PTT uses circuit switched transmission, while PoC utilizes a digital packet radio and Internet Protocol technologies. PoC though shows poor commercial adoption, which is partly because the standardisation process is still ongoing (Ali-Vehmas & Luukkainen, 2008). Currently, some smart phones (e.g., Motorola i1 Android, BlackBerry Curve, iPhone) provide push to talk capabilities. Interconnecting the roadies via a PTT or PoC system enhances the communication and eases coordination of tasks in real-time.

4.3.3 Organising musicians

Organising the musicians is a process that can be profoundly supported by technology. The basic idea is to build a system with a Web interface that can automatically react to users' responses. Figure 19 illustrates the improved process.

In the first step, the manager has to insert the information on the event, which he has sent via e-mail up to now, into the database. For each recipient, he may (or may not) create a personalised paragraph for the e-mail.

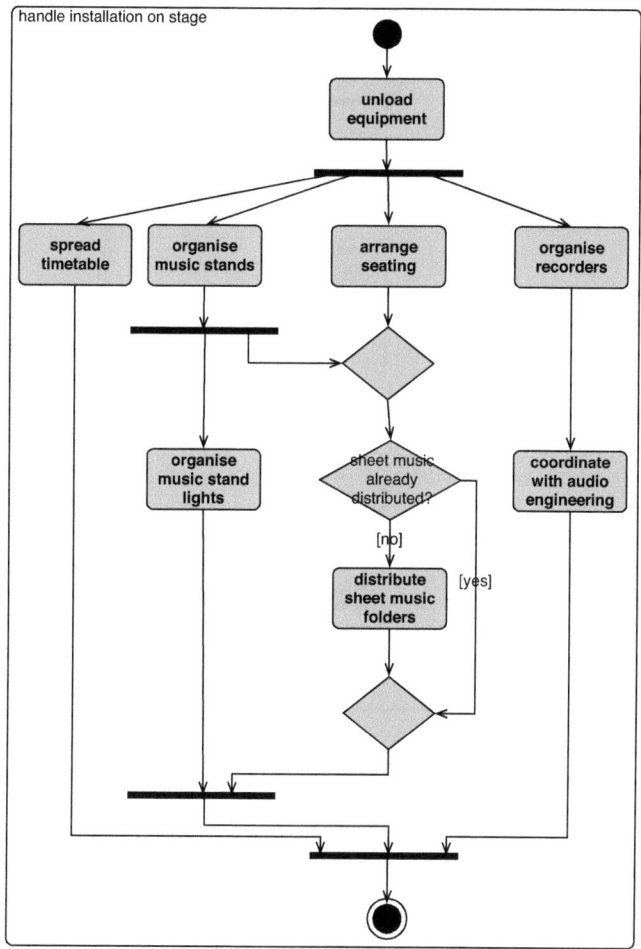

Figure 17. UML activity diagram for the improved process of handling the installation on stage

Simultaneously, he sets up a Web form, where the musicians can indicate whether they will participate at the event.

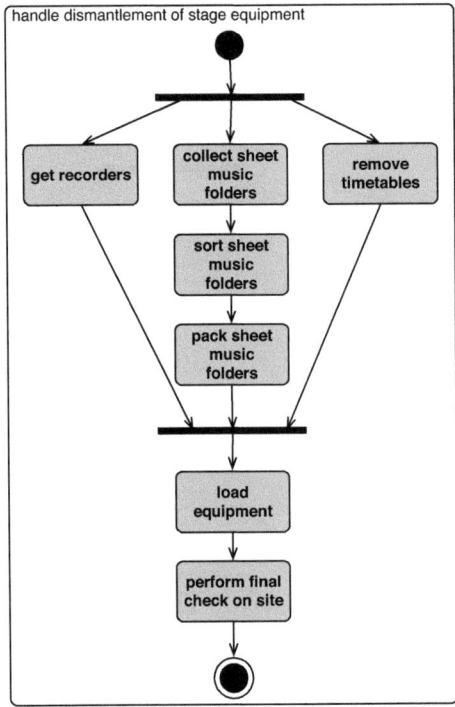

Figure 18. UML activity diagram for the improved process of handling the dismantlement of stage equipment

Then he runs a script that automatically sends e-mails to the musicians that contains the standard information from the database and the personalised paragraph, depending on the addressee.

Then the system can manage the responses. As soon as a musician indicates on the Web form whether he or she will participate, the system reacts. If a musician answers that he or she cannot participate, the system automatically creates and submits an e-mail to the respective understudy. If the understudy cannot participate, then the manager organises an alternative. If after a particular set time period, there are still answers missing, the manager calls those musicians who have not replied. If the band is still not complete, he organises alternative players for the respective instruments.

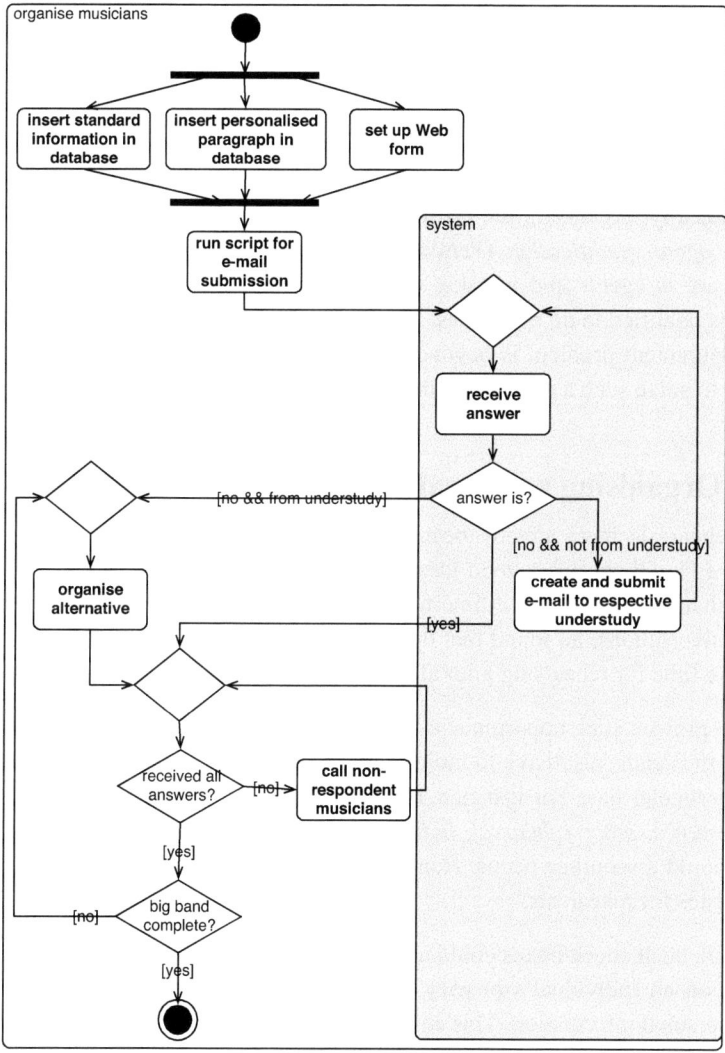

Figure 19. UML activity diagram for the improved process for organising musicians

This scenario allows the manager to be highly supported by technology while maintaining a personalised touch. First, he can send a personalised message. Second, he may call specific individuals via phone (for instance, when a person is either not Internet-literate or particularly important to the band) and use the Web form to answer for an individual when needed.

If process optimisation is the goal though, only Internet-literate people should be included in the pool of possible musicians. Because musicians tend to be replaceable in a *telephone band*, Internet-literacy could be an additional criterion for *recruitment,* besides musical skills.

Basically, organising the musicians is a *classic assignment problem recognizing agent qualification* (Pentico, 2007) as known in operations research. There are m agents and n tasks, where n is less than m. However, not every agent is qualified to do every task. The objective is utility maximisation. Solving this assignment problem is beyond the scope of this work. For a mathematical model to solve such a problem with side constraints, see Caron et al. (1999).

4.3.4 Organising rehearsals

The rehearsals have already been organised with the support of technology. Using a Doodle poll is a good idea. Still, the manager claimed that people indicated that they do not have time for rehearsal on a certain day. During one-on-one conversations, he found that they frequently do not have sound reasons and do have time for rehearsing after all.

To prevent such opportunistic behaviour, it could help to adopt a Web form where musicians also have to indicate the reasons for not being able to rehearse on a particular day. For instance, the Web form could provide check boxes for *performance, other rehearsal, holiday, private,* or something similar. This priming could discourage people from lying. As a result, it would be easier to find joint dates for rehearsals.

Still, such check boxes could also have a negative effect because it could infringe on an individual's privacy. People may feel uncomfortable to disclose such personal information. This could also damage the manager's image for asking for such information, so before adopting such a tool, it would be advisable to survey people's attitudes towards disclosing such information.

4.3.5 Organising sheet music

As already mentioned in the introduction to Section 4.3, one should reconsider the real value of presenting new self-made arrangements every year. On the one hand, presenting new arrangements is a musical asset of VBO and could be its unique selling proposition (USP). On the other hand, this task is complex and time consuming.

Yet handling sheet music can also be supported by information technology. A still rarely used device is the *digital music stand* (Graefe, Wahila, Maguire, & Dasna, 1996; Kumarova, 2007). Instead of presenting sheet music on paper, it is shown on a display. By using technology support, additional features, such as page turning, music management, or tuning, become possible (Graefe, et al., 1996).

For sheet music management, digital music stands are advantageous because sheet music can be loaded and spread to the instruments' music stands with the click of a button. Handling sheet music on paper takes hours because the security copies for every instrument's part need to be made and then sorted into each sheet music folder.

Adopting digital music stands for a band can have disadvantages though. First of all, it involves a high initial investment, as 22 digital music stands would have to be bought. Second, musicians – and *telephone musicians* in particular – are used to making manual annotations directly onto the sheet music. Although some digital music stands support annotations (e.g., Graefe, et al., 1996), this feature is not yet sophisticated enough to substitute pencil-and-paper annotations. Third, and this is a major problem, there is the risk of system failure. If there is a technical problem and the system fails, there is not any other sheet music available. Without sheet music, the band cannot play at all, which is a severe problem for the entire event. Fourth, available systems restrict the band to sheet mu-sic that is compatible with the system. The favoured arrangements are thus not available for the digital music stand system. Furthermore, self-made arrangements, which are an asset for any big band, will not be system-compliant. Of the few professional music notation softwares (e.g., Sibelius, Finale) that exist, none of them can export music to digital music stand systems. Even if music stand systems support the import of midi-files, which music notation software supports, annotations, which are software-specific, get lost in this crucial process. Accordingly, midi-support is not sufficient for professional use.

In conclusion, digital music stands in their current developmental state are not sophisticated enough to be adopted in practise, so it is advisable to keep the common paper sheet music system.

4.3.6 Creating the set list and submitting the song list to the collecting society

The set list and the song list for the collecting society[9] are strongly interlinked, as the latter has to have the songs that have been played at a certain event. Basically creating and submitting the song list to the collecting society is an easy task. Still, it is time-consuming and for many people, *annoying*.

With the support of a script, the set list can be rather easily translated into the song list for the collecting society. This requires a database where the songs' meta-data are stored. Figure 20 presents an entity relationship diagram for the entire database.

The song table includes the attributes title, composer, lyricist, arranger, index number in the sheet music folders, and whether it is performed as a vocal or instrumental song. For the set list, the title and index number are sufficient. The song list for the collecting society requires all the song information except the index number.

The table for location contains address data with postcode, street, town and country. An event is always related to a certain location, although there could be several events on one location. For instance, there could be a ball upstairs and a club downstairs in a venue, with each having a different organiser.

An event is represented by id, event name, and date. For each event, there is at least one set list that contains at least one song (i.e. an event without a set list cannot exist, and a set list without song cannot exist).

Every set list is associated with one specific event. The table set list has an id as the primary key. It contains the songs' indices and the event's id as foreign

---

[9] A collecting society is an organisation that has the authority to license copyrighted works and collect royalties on behalf of the copyright owners.

keys. For the songs, the attribute song sequence represents the rank number in the sequence, where one song could occur several times in a set list.

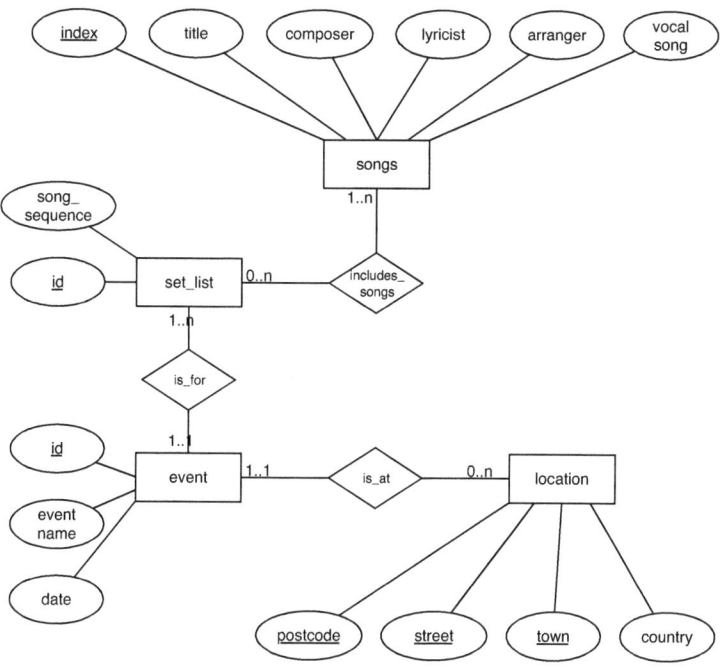

Figure 20. Entity relationship diagram for the song database

At the venue, the musicians and the manager need to be able to view the songs for a particular event sorted by song sequence. The song list should contain the column song title and have the header naming the title of the event.

The song list for the collecting society needs to additionally contain information on when the song is being played. It has to contain all meta-data on the songs except the index. The meta-data includes the event name, the date, and the full address of where the events took place. Every song can only be listed once, and for each song, the number of times each song was played has to be given.

4.3.7 Providing payment

As already mentioned in the introduction to this section (Section 4.3), to make the payment process easier and less stressful, the manager could prepare the fee notes before the event (Figure 21).

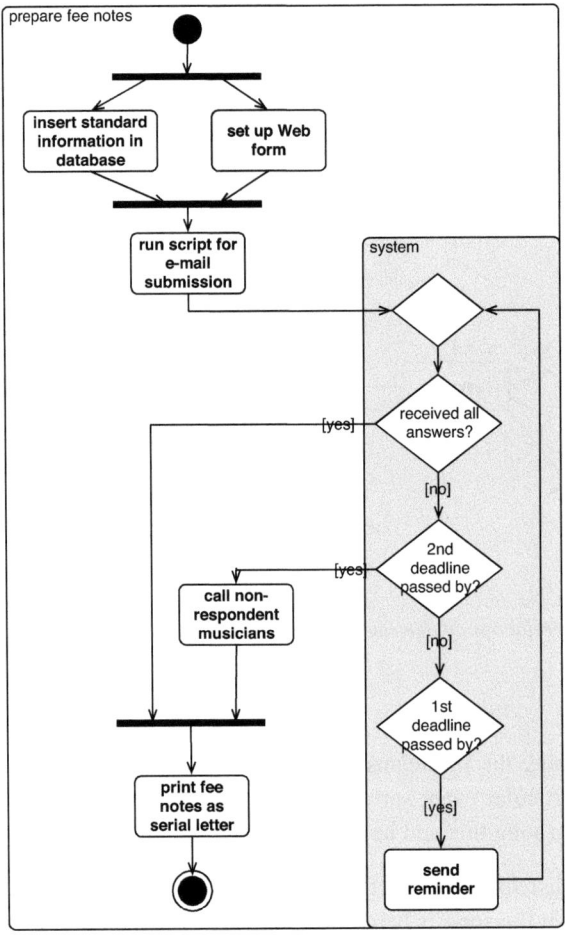

Figure 21. UML activity diagram for preparing fee notes

To prepare the fee notes, every musician's full name and address are needed. For musicians who are entitled to input tax deduction, also the value-added tax (VAT) number is required. To obtain this information, the manager could send a mass e-mail to the musicians using standard text. This e-mail would include a link to a prepared Web form, where musicians are asked to insert their names, addresses, and optionally their VAT numbers.

If some musicians have not responded after a certain predefined deadline, the system automatically sends the musicians a reminder. If there are still answers missing after a second deadline, the manager can then phone those musicians to provide their information. As soon as all musicians have responded, the fee notes may be printed with the provided data, using the series letter functionality.

Instead of providing blank fee note forms after the event, the fee notes would then already be filled in. The musicians would just have to sign the completed fee notes. As the manager has prepared the forms by himself, he can be sure that the data is correct. Then, he just has to check the signature (Figure 22).

A combined bank transfer is also a possible alternative to cash payment, even though cash is preferred among musicians. In the process depicted in Figure 21, the Web form could additionally ask for the bank account details, since this information is required for transferring the money. The process depicted in Figure 22 would change the payment process in the following way: Instead of paying the compensation, the manager would only collect the fee notes. A couple of days after the event, he would arrange for a combined bank transfer using the online payment facilities at his bank institution.

Although the processes are quite similar, the bank transfer has a distinctive advantage over cash payment. Because payment involves such a considerable sum of money, it can be risky to carry that money in cash to the event. When opting for the bank transfer, the organiser may be asked to transfer the full amount to the bank account instead of using cash. Then, the manager does not have to take the risk of carrying that money around with him.

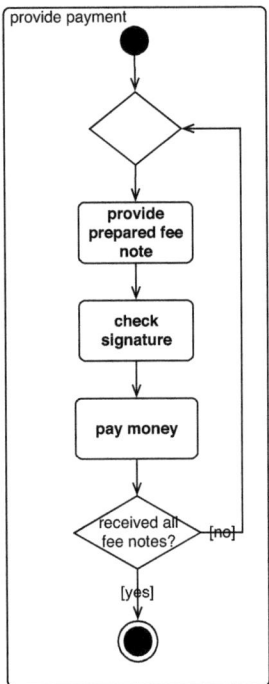

Figure 22. UML activity diagram for improving the process of payment

4.3.8 Final check at the venue

Performing the final check at the venue manually is frequently cumbersome and holds the risk of forgetting something at the venue. Radio frequency identification (RFID) (Ahson & Ilyas, 2008) may remedy the situation.

RFID provides the ability to collect raw data about objects, location and status (International Telecommunication Union, 2005). The primary benefit of RFID systems is the ability to capture data without the necessity for line-of-sight between RFID reader and the object (Lampe, Floerkemeier, & Haller, 2005). There are three types of RFID tags. Passive tags do not have power source and require an external electromagnetic field to initiate signal transmission. Active RFID tags, in contrast, contain a battery and can transmit signals once an external source has been successfully identified. Finally, there are battery-assisted passive tags (semi-passive) tags, which require an external source (interrogator; RFID reader) to wake up. The read ranges vary on the type of RFID system used (i.e., passive vs. active, operating frequencies, etc.) as well as the surrounding environment (i.e., indoor vs. outdoor, metal, liquids, etc.). However, typical transmission ranges have been found between a few centimetres for passive and up to one hundred meters for semi-passive and active tags (Ahson & Ilyas, 2008).

The basic idea is to equip all physical resources of the band with (semi-passive) RFID tags. Using a handheld RFID reader, the car loaded with the band's equipment can be scanned. The scan will reveal whether all resources are already inside the car or if one or more items are missing. Particularly it also provides information on which items are missing. Having that information, the main areas where the band stayed (stage, backstage, hallway) can be scanned using the RFID reader in order to locate the missing items.

Using RFID-support, the process itself remains quite similar to the one without RFID. Still risk of loss may be reduced significantly. Furthermore, locating missing items will be less cumbersome and time-consuming due to RFID's ability to locate items.

5. Discussion and outlook

Previous sections demonstrate the complexity of the processes involved in managing a *telephone band*. Equally, Section 4.3 identifies the advantages of adopting technologies in the entire process.

This section tries to collate findings from the case study discussed in Section 4 and derive recommendations that can be adopted for the management of (telephone) bands generally.

5.1 Interpretation of results

While some processes – such as the organisation of the musicians – is specific to the management of a *telephone band*, other processes are also transferable to organic bands. Particularly the chronological sequence of the general process of managing the band for the event can be considered generic and can hence be the basis for band management generally.

Knowledge sharing is a particularly important factor affecting a band's success. By placing the majority of the burden on the manger, the failure or success of the show depends on one individual. If he or she, for instance, gets ill, there would not be an alternative solution. As a consequence, it is crucial to either have an additional person understand all the processes and manager's responsibilities or to scatter the knowledge and responsibilities among many people. Furthermore, we have to consider that as the focal company in the virtual organisation, the manager has to assume full contractual liability to the event organiser. To fulfil this obligation, knowledge sharing seems to be the safest approach.

By structuring and documenting the entire process, the process itself becomes more efficient. As the processes involve partly tacit knowledge, it is particularly important to make this knowledge explicit so that others can build on it by applying the existing knowledge or by adapting and improving that knowledge. This work – in particular Section 4 – represents an approach in structuring the activities and making tacit knowledge explicit and easily understandable to others.

In any case, a certain willingness towards division of labour and knowledge sharing is necessary to diminish the risk of putting all the metaphorical eggs into one basket. This does not only refer to division of labour among people but also to the adoption of technology. Trust in technology is essential in order to fully leverage technology-supported processes. If the involved persons (e.g., the manager and the musicians) do not show a certain degree of trust towards technology and the people *behind* the technology, they must invest in developing trust before technology can be successfully deployed.

Concerning technologies, it seems practical to adopt them in the early stages of the entire process. As shown in earlier sections, sub-processes frequently depend on preceding processes and activities. If information is already available in digital form, such as the musicians' contact details, then it is easy to use this information in several subsequent activities, such as informing them about rehearsals in an e-mail or using the contact information to prepare fee notes. Collecting and preparing information electronically may sometimes be inefficient for one-time uses because it takes up resources and is often time-consuming. So, the more activities that benefit from this one-time investment within the entire process, the more advantageous it is to adopt the technology. Still, it is important to keep in mind that the adoption of technology may yield a benefit only after having gone through the entire process several times. In other words, sometimes the additional activities and costs involved with the adoption of new technologies have to be regarded as long-term investments that are profitable after several years of application only. The earlier the move towards technology, the earlier one can benefit from its advantages and the bigger the profit one might expect for future use.

Still, before adopting process improvements, one has to consider domain-specific conventions, rules, and activities. The theoretical increase of process performance does not necessarily lead to an operational process improvement because domain-specific hurdles may hamper the full potential of the theoretical improvement.

For instance, operational details on how sheet music is used on stage relates to why existing electronic music stands have failed to reach business success. The knowledge that musicians frequently make notes on sheet music before playing a song is a significant detail. For a *rented* musician who has never seen certain sheet music before, it is particularly important to grasp the structure of the song immediately. Consequently, repetitions and key changes are frequently highlighted on scores. Because this has to work instantly and quickly, it is most convenient to use a pencil to accentuate the respective passages in the sheet music. This *quick and dirty* solution is so useful that other mediums without a highlighting process have not been adopted by the users, i.e., musicians.

Another prominent example is that musicians are commonly paid immediately after a performance. This fact must not be neglected when changing the processes that affect payment. It would be advantageous for many reasons to use a combined bank transfer for paying the musicians. First, it would reduce the risk of theft involved when having a large amount of money on oneself. Second, it decreases the risk of paying the wrong amounts of money from miscalculations. Third, it diminishes the stress adding additional tasks on at already stressful time because transferring the money can be postponed to the subsequent day. Still the convention and expectation is that payment will be given on the day of the performance. Process improvements can only be performed as long as they consider this convention.

Finally, it is advisable for the manager to try to provide a more accurate image of himself to those he works with. It appears that musicians as well as involved special guests and artists view the manager primarily as a *conductor*. Yet, as a manager taking over responsibility for a number of organisational tasks as well as handling any kind of coordination regarding the stage, including special guests and artists, the role as a *manager* should be emphasised. A central task should be to work on being regarded as a *manager* rather than just the conductor of the band. This role should be clear to and accepted by each member of the virtual organisation (e.g., musicians, vocalists, roadies).

5.2 Future research

The research presented in this work provides substantial findings that support the management of *telephone bands* through tapping the potential of technology in improving their organisational processes. More than that, results are applicable to many different types of band or artist management. Furthermore, findings may support any kind of event organisation (e.g., music, sports, political, and entertainment events, conferences, congresses, shows), covering events as small as company parties to ones as big as the Olympic games. Beyond, the management of virtual organisation may profit from the findings on ICT-support of a *telephone band*'s processes.

Still, this work is one of the first examinations into this field, so there are many aspects that still require further research. In particular, the following issues stand out as prominent ideas for future research endeavours:

- One of the goals of this work was to capture the complexity involved in managing *telephone bands*. A first approach was to capture, document, and analyse activities in a case study. While the case study research strategy is an adequate means to answer the raised research questions, its scope for generalisation is limited. Consequently, it seems advisable to perform further case studies with similar *telephone bands* for similar events. With multiple case studies, comparisons can be undertaken, revealing commonalities and differences. Although the VBO was selected for the case study, under the assumption that it was a *typical* telephone band, only further analysis can provide validation.

- A logical step after providing suggestions to improve processes on a conceptual basis is to implement this work's findings. The impact of the new processes on performance would either validate or disprove this research's findings. Here, particularly two effects appear interesting. First, a recommended research objective is to analyse the impact of the implemented new processes on process performance. Do the new processes require fewer resources? Do they involve less time? What is the impact on people concerning division of labour and the expansion of the roadies' responsibilities? Moreover, it seems relevant to investigate whether changes in payment could be implemented with a positive response from musicians. Do the new processes involve less risk? Second, it is also necessary to investigate the impact of the new processes on the artistic performance. The artistic output of a band must maintain quality performances. If the artistic performance suffers such that the audience can perceive a difference, the improved processes are counterintuitive to the success of the band. Consequently, the processes, which have been suggested by this work, need to be validated in further research, both concerning the process' performance and the band's artistic performance.

- A further challenge in implementing these new processes is to choose either a gradual adoption of technologies (incremental innovation) or a disruptive innovation by completely rearranging all processes at once. This decision has to be carefully considered by the management as any kind of change also impacts an organisation's culture. With a disruptive innovation, the involved persons may resist the changes and subsequently, create a negative environment for everyone. As a consequence, this would negatively impact the whole performance of the band. On the other hand, even adopting an incremental approach, people could still be reluctant to adopt new innovations. While accepting the first few innovations, they might resist to further changes. This would result in an only partially implemented solution. Accordingly, it is up to further research to investigate which way would be most appropriate for the involved target group.

- Next, this work deliberately selected a *telephone big band* for its case study in order to ensure the complexity of processes involved since a big band involves a relatively large number of people. Questions that remain unanswered are the following: At what size does an organisation get good returns for using technology? What other characteristics affect the exploitation of technology's benefits (e.g., involved risk, resources, venue)? This work could show that not only the sub-processes that involve many people are complex and could profit from technology-support but also that other sub-processes could benefit. Accordingly, one may hypothesise that a large part of the improved processes could also be of use to smaller bands. Still, it is an issue of interest to investigate at what band size technology-support is appropriate.

- A further major question concerns the technological literacy of musicians. As this work reveals, there is a number of (even young) musicians that are not computer-literate. Adopting technology in processes may be an insurmountable obstacle, if many of the users are not computer-literate. This raises the question of whether a basic technological training should also be part of artistic curricula. Research has shown (for details see Bauer, et al., 2011) that managerial skills are hardly implemented in current artistic curricula in the German-speaking area (so-called DACH countries). Similar to Bauer et al. (2011), future research should analyse whether technological topics are addressed in curricula and what impact an implementation of technological courses could have on the everyday activities of musicians. This work hypothesises that a thorough education and training of musicians in technological skills would lead to an improved and efficient deployment of technology. This hypothesis is grounded on the argument that a whole process could fail because an individual does not possess relevant computer skills.

- In addition, the concept of a *telephone band* could be subject to more in-depth investigation, concerning the phenomenon of virtual organisations. This work focused on the internal processes of the *telephone band* with a particular view to the role of the bandleader (focal company). Future research could investigate the formation processes analogous to the work of Haas (2007). Haas (2007) investigated the formation processes of SME networks. Furthermore, it would be interesting to analyse the liabilities, risks, and interests of the participating organisation partners.

Overall, this work provides insights on what tool designers need to take into consideration when developing tools that support the processes of managing virtual organisations and *telephone bands* in particular. Translating these findings into tangible tool requirements and specifications resulting in supportive tools would be one of the next steps to be taken.

6. Summary

This work presented the processes involved in managing a *telephone band* and suggested measures for improvement with particular view to the application of information and communication technologies.

The first section explained the motivation behind this research endeavour based on following assumptions:

- The processes of managing a band are not transparent to a wider public because of a lack of research and education in the field.

- Managing a *telephone band* involves complex processes, while the management of medium-sized bands are more complex than managing smaller ones.

- The efficient use of information and communication technologies (ICT) is rare in managing bands and orchestras.

- The adoption of ICT may improve the processes involved.

The second section presented theory and background of the constructs underlying this work in order to provide the reader with adequate background information. First, the difference between artists and artisans was discussed. Second, the various types of bands were defined. Third, the activities and duties of musicians as one-person enterprises were discussed. Finally, the section gave an overview the *telephone band* as virtual organisation.

The third section is dedicated to the methods adopted for this research endeavour. Research strategies that are commonly used in the interdisciplinary field related to the social sciences were presented. In particular, research methodology commonly adopted in business informatics was presented. Based on these considerations, the most appropriate research strategy was selected for approaching this work's research questions: the case study strategy. Next, this section presented the case study design with a thorough documentation of the research process. Furthermore, the language definition for the visualisation of the processes was selected (UML 2.3 standard for activity diagrams) and described in detail. Additionally, the SWOT analysis was outlined.

As the main contribution of this work, the fourth section presented the case study. This section comprised three parts. First, the current situation was outlined in detail, both visually and verbally. Second, a SWOT analysis was performed, highlighting the strengths, weaknesses, opportunities, and threats of the current situation of the processes involved. Third, suggestions for process improvements were given with particular consideration to ICT.

Bringing the findings together, the fifth section presented conclusions and recommendations for the operationalising processes involved in managing *telephone bands*. Similarities to the management of organic bands were emphasised.

Finally the sixth section pinpointed unanswered questions and suggested fields for future research.

7. References

Ahson, Syed & Ilyas, Mohammad (Eds.) (2008). *RFID Handbook: Applications, Technology, Security, and Privacy*. Boca Raton, FL: CRC Press.

Ali-Vehmas, Timo & Luukkainen, Sakari (2008). Service adoption strategies of push over cellular. *Personal and Ubiquitous Computing, 12*(1), 35-44. doi: 10.1007/s00779-006-0122-3.

Allen, Paul (2007). *Artist management for the music business*. Amsterdam, The Netherlands, Boston, Massachusetts: Elsevier/Focal Press.

Amason, Allen C. (2010). *Strategic management: from theory to practice*. London, United Kingdom: Routledge.

Andrews, Chris (2009). *SWOT: The Evolution Of IT Service Providers To Business Technology Competitors: The Business Technology Offerings Of Accenture, Capgemini, Cognizant, And IBM*. Forrester Research, Cambridge, Massachusetts.

Angrosino, Michael V. (2009). *Doing ethnographic and observational research*. London: Sage Publications.

Bauer, Christine, Viola, Katharina, & Strauss, Christine (2011). Management skills for artists: 'learning by doing'? *International Journal of Cultural Policy*. doi: 10.1080/10286632.2010.531716.

Beckman, Svante (2001). *Conditions for Creative Artists in Europe: Report from the EU Presidency Seminar in Visby (Sweden)*. Ministry of Culture, Sweden, Visby, Sweden.

Bernroider, Edward (2002). Factors in SWOT Analysis Applied to Micro, Small-to-Medium, and Large Software Enterprises: an Austrian Study. *European Management Journal, 20*(5), 562-573. doi: 10.1016/S0263-237 3(02)00095-6.

Bolan, Sandra (2002). Artists Need Business Know-How. *Computing Canada, 28*(7).

BonbonBall (2010). *Website of the BonbonBall*. Retrieved 23 September 2010, from http://www.bonbonball.at/.

Bundesministerium für Wirtschaft und Technologie (2009). *Informationen zur Existenzgründung und -sicherung: Thema: Existenzgründungstipps für Künstler und Publizisten.* BMWi, Berlin.

Caron, Gaétan, Hansen, Pierri, & Jaumard, Brigitte (1999). The assignment problem with seniority and job priority constraints. *Operations Research, 47*(3).

Chen, Peter Pin-shan (1976). The Entity-Relationship Model: Toward a Unified View of Data. *ACM Transactions on Database Systems, 1*(1), 9-36. doi: 10.1.1.123.1085.

Child, John & Faulkner, David (1998). *Strategies of cooperation: managing alliances, networks, and joint ventures.* Oxford, United Kingdom: Oxford University Press.

Clement, Michel, Papies, Dominik, & Schusser, Oliver (Eds.) (2008). *Ökonomie der Musikindustrie* (2nd ed.). Wiesbaden, Germany: Gabler.

Clulow, Val (2005). Futures dilemmas for marketers: can stakeholder analysis add value? *European Journal of Marketing, 39*(9/10), 978-997. doi: 10.11 08/03090560510610671.

Colbert, François (2003). Entrepreneurship and Leadership in Marketing the Arts. *Marketing Management, 6*(1), 30-39.

Council of Europe & European Institute for Comparative Cultural Research (ERICarts) (2010). *Quick Facts: Switzerland. Compendium of Cultural Policies and Trends in Europe.* Retrieved 08 June 2010, from http://www.culturalpolicies.net/web/countries.php?pcid=1460.

Dangel, Caroline, Piorkowsky, Michael-Burkhard, & Stamm, Thomas (2006). *Selbstständige Künstlerinnen und Künstler in Deutschland - zwischen brotloser Kunst und freiem Unternehmertum?* Deutscher Kulturrat, Berlin, Germany.

Davidow, William H. & Malone, Michael S. (1992). *The virtual corporation: structuring and revitalizing the corporation for the 21st century.* New York, NY: Harper Collins.

Deutscher Bundestag (2007). *Schlussbericht der Enquete-Kommission "Kultur in Deutschland".* Deutscher Bundestag, 16. Wahlperiode. Berlin.

Dudek, Stephanie Z., Bernèche, René, Bérubé, Huguette, & Royer, Sylvie (1991). Personality determinants of the commitment to the profession of art *Creativity Research Journal, 4*(4), 367-389. doi: 10.1080/10400419109534412.

Eikhof, Doris Ruth & Haunschild, Axel (2007). For art's sake! Artistic and economic logics in creative production. *Journal of Organizational Behavior, 28*(7), 523-538. doi: 10.1002/job.462.

Engh, Marcel (2006). *Popstars als Marke: Identitätsorientiertes Markenmanagement für die musikindustrielle Künstlerentwicklung und -vermarktung.* Wiesbaden, Germany: Gabler.

Engh, Marcel (2008). Managing Artists and Repertoire (A&R). In Clement, Michel, Papies, Dominik, & Schusser, Oliver (Eds.), *Ökonomie der Musikindustrie* (pp. 99-116). Wiesbaden, Germany: Gabler.

European Institute for Comparative Cultural Research (ERICarts) (2006). *The status of artists in Europe.* IP/B/CULT/ST/2005-89. Directorate General Internal Policies of the Union, Brussels, Belgium.

Fenderich, Laurie (2005). A Portrait of the Artist as a Young Mess. *Chronicle of Higher Education, 51*(29), B6-B8.

Fink, Michael (1996). *Inside the music industry: creativity, process, and business* (2nd ed.). New York, NY: Schirmer Books.

Flick, Uwe, Kardorff, Ernst von, Keupp, Heiner, Rosenstiel, Lutz von, & Wolff, Stephan (Eds.) (1995). *Handbuch Qualitative Sozialforschung: Grundlagen, Konzepte, Methoden und Anwendungen* (2nd ed.). Weinheim, Germany: Beltz Psychologie-Verlags-Union.

Frascogna, Xavier M. & Hetherington, H. Lee (2004). *This business of artist management* (4th ed.). New York, NY: Billboard Books.

Frey, Bruno S. & Pommerehne, Werner W. (1989). *Muses and Markets: Explorations in the Economics of the Arts.* Oxford, United Kingdom: Basil Blackwell.

Frost, Frederick A. (2003). The use of strategic tools by small and medium-sized enterprises: an Australasian study. *Strategic Change, 12*, 49-62. doi: 10.1002/jsc.607.

Gensch, Gerhard, Stöckler, Eva Maria, & Tschmuck, Peter (2009). *Musikrezeption, Musikdistribution und Musikproduktion: Der Wandel des Wertschöpfungsnetzwerks in der Musikwirtschaft*. Wiesbaden, Germany: Gabler.

Ginsburgh, Victor A. & Throsby, David (Eds.) (2006). *Handbook of the economics of art and culture*. Amsterdam, The Netherlands: North Holland.

Glaister, Keith W. & Falshaw, J. Richard (1999). Strategic Planning: Still Going Strong? *Long Range Planning, 32*(1), 107-116. doi: 10.1016/S0024-6301(98)00131-9.

Goulding, Christina (2005). Grounded theory, ethnography and phenomenology: A comparative analysis of three qualitative strategies for marketing research. *European Journal of Marketing, 39*(3/4), 294-308.

Graefe, Christopher, Wahila, Derek, Maguire, Justin, & Dasna, Orya (1996). Designing the muse: a digital music stand for the symphony musician. Proceeedings of the *CHI 1996*, 13-18 April 1996, Vancouver, Canada.

Haak, Caroll (2005). *Künstler zwischen selbständiger und unabhängiger Erwerbsarbeit. Discussion paper. Wissenschaftszentrum Berlin für Sozialforschung. Berlin*. SP I 2005-107. Wissenschaftszentrum Berlin für Sozialforschung (WZB), Berlin, Germany.

Haas, Marita (2007). *The formation process of SME networks: a comparative case analysis of social processes in Austria, Belgium and Turkey*. Wiesbaden, Germany: Deutscher Universitäts-Verlag (DUV).

Hammersley, Martyn & Gomm, Roger (2000). Introduction. In Gomm, Roger, Hammersley, Martyn, & Foster, Peter (Eds.), *Case Study Method: Key Issues, Key Texts* (pp. 1-16). London, Thousand Oaks, New Delhi: Sage Publications.

Helfferich, Cornelia (2005). *Die Qualität qualitativer Daten: Manual für die Durchführung qualitativer Interviews* (2nd ed.). Wiesbaden, Germany: Verlag für Sozialwissenschaften (VS).

Hevner, Alan R., March, Salvatore T., Park, Jinsoo, & Ram, Sudha (2004). Design Science in Information System Research. *MIS Quarterly, 28*(1), 75-105.

Hill, Terry & Westbrook, Roy (1997). SWOT analysis: It's time for a product recall. *Long Range Planning, 30*(1), 46-52. doi: 10.1016/S0024-6301(96)00095-7.

Hycner, Richard H. (1985). Some guidelines for the phenomenological analysis of interview data. *Human Studies, 8*, 279-303.

International Telecommunication Union (2005). *The Internet of Things* (7th ed.). Geneva: International Telecommunication Union.

Jansen, Brigitte E. S. & Simon, Jürgen W. (2008). *Virtuelle Unternehmenskooperationen: Rechtliche und strategische Instrumente zur Implementierung*. Munich, Germany: Akademischer Verlag München (AVM).

Jorgensen, Danny L. (1999). *Participant observation: a methodology for human studies*. Newbury Park, CA: Sage Publications.

Karttunen, Sari (1998). How to identify artists?: Defining the population for 'status-of-the-artist' studies. *Poetics, 26*(1), 1-19. doi: 10.1016/S0304-422X(98)00007-2.

Ko, Ryain K. L., Lee, Stephen S. G., & Lee, Eng Wah (2009). Business process management (BPM) standards: a survey. *Business Process Management Journal, 15*(5), 744-791. doi: 10.1108/14637150910987937.

Köszegi, Sabine (2001). *Vertrauen in virtuellen Unternehmen*. Wiesbaden, Germany: Deutscher Universitäts-Verlag (DUV).

Kubacki, Krzysztof & Croft, Robin (2005). Paying the piper: a study of musicians and the music business. *International Journal of Nonprofit and Voluntary Sector Marketing, 10*(4), 225-236. doi: 10.1002/nvsm.27.

Kulle, Jürgen (1998). *Ökonomie der Musikindustrie: eine Analyse der körperlichen und unkörperlichen Musikverwertung mit Hilfe von Tonträgern und Netzen*. Frankfurt, Germany: Peter Lang.

Kumarova, Myra Gabbasovna (2007). *Digital music stand*. United States Patent No. US 2007/0175316 A1.

La Valle, Ivana, O'Regan, Siobhan, & Jackson, Charles (2000). *The Art of Getting Started: Graduate skills in a fragmented labour market* (Vol. IES Report 364). London, UK: Grantham Book Services.

Lampe, Matthias, Floerkemeier, Christian, & Haller, Stephan (2005). Einführung in die RFID-Technologie. In Fleisch, Elgar & Mattern, Friedemann (Eds.), *Das Internet der Dinge: Ubiquitous Computing und RFID in der Praxis* (pp. 279-290). Berlin: Springer.

Lathrop, Tad & Pettigrew, Jim (2003). *This business of music marketing & promotion* (2nd revised and updated ed.). New York, NY: Billboard Books.

Leinenbach, Stefan (2000). *Interaktive Geschäftsprozessmodellierung: Dokumentation von Prozesswissen in einer virtual-reality-gestützten Unternehmungsvisualisierung.* Wiesbaden: Deutscher Universitätsverlag (DUV).

Menger, Pierre-Michel (1999). Artistic Labor Markets and Careers. *Annual Review of Sociology, 25*, 541-574. doi: 10.1146/annurev.soc.25.1.541.

Menger, Pierre-Michel (2001). Artists as workers: Theoretical and methodological challenges. *Poetics, 28*(4), 241-254. doi: 10.1016/S0304-422X(01)800 02-4.

Merriam, Sharan B. (1988). *Case study research in education: A qualitative approach.* San Francisco, CA, London, United Kingdom: Jossey-Bass.

Mertens, Peter (1998). *Virtuelle Unternehmen und Informationsverarbeitung.* Berlin, Germany: Springer.

Miles, Matthew B. & Huberman, A. Michael (1994). *Qualitative data analysis: an expanded sourcebook* (2nd ed.). Thousand Oakes, London, New Delhi: Sage Publications.

Montag Stiftung Bildende Kunst Bonn, Akademie der bildenen Künste Wien, & Verlag für moderne Kunst (2008). Job Descriptions: KünstlerInnen in einer veränderten Berufswelt. Proceeedings of the *3. Symposium der Reihe "Heraus aus dem Elfenbeinturm!"*2008, Nürnberg, Germany.

Moussetis, Robert & Ernst, Glary (2004). The Artist as an Entrepreneur: An Exploratory Study and Propositions. Proceeedings of the *USASBE/SBI 2004 Joint Conference*, 14-20 January 2004, Dallas, TX.

Music Council of Australia (MCA) (2009). *Analyses of strengths, weaknesses, opportunities and threats in the Australian music sector. Music in Austra-*

lia Knowledge Base. Retrieved 2 January 2009, from http://www.mca.org. au/web/component/option,com_kb/task,article/article,7/.

N. N. (2008, 16 September 2008). Double Fourtime Dixiband: Jazz: Musik für jeden Zweck, *Wochenpost,* p. 23. Retrieved 29 December 2009 from http://www.leichlinger-stadtfest.de/cmsneu/images/wochenpost08/woposo nderausgabe_08_Seite23.pdf.

North, Michael (Ed.) (1996). *Economic history and the arts*. Köln, Germany: Böhlau.

O'del, John (2003). Entrepreneurship in the Arts: Toward an Educational Approach. Proceeedings of the *USASBE/SBI 2003 Joint Conference*, 23-26 January 2003, Hilton Head, SC.

Object Management Group (2010a). *Business Process Model And Notation (BPMN)*. Retrieved 26 October 2010, from http://www.omg.org/spec/BP MN/.

Object Management Group (2010b). *OMG Unified Modeling Lanugage™ (OMG UML), Superstructure, Version 2.3*. Retrieved 1 January 2011, from http://www.omg.org/spec/UML/2.3/Superstructure/PDF/.

Peng, Guo Chao Alex & Nunes, Migual Baptista (2007). Using PEST analysis as a tool for refining and focusing contexts for information systems research. Proceeedings of the *6th European Conference on Research Methodology for Business and Management Studies*, 9-10 July 2007, Lisbon, Portugal.

Pentico, David W. (2007). Assignment problems: A golden anniversary survey. *European Journal of Operational Research, 176*, 774-793.

Picot, Arnold, Reichwald, Ralf, & Wigand, Rolf T. (2003). *Die grenzenlose Unternehmung* (5th, updated ed.). Wiesbaden, Germany: Gabler.

Röttgers, Janko (2003). *Mix, burn & R.I.P.: das Ende der Musikindustrie*. Hannover, Germany: Heise.

Røyseng, Sigrid, Mangset, Per, & Borgen, Jorunn Spord (2007). Young Artists and the Charismatic Myth. *International Journal of Cultural Policy, 13*(1), 1-16. doi: 10.1080/10286630600613366.

Schelepa, Susanne, Wetzel, Petra, & Wohlfahrt, Gerhard (2008). *Zur sozialen Lage der Künstler und Künstlerinnen in Österreich: Endbericht*. L & R Social Research, Wien, Austria.

Schneider, Beate & Weinacht, Stefan (Eds.) (2007). *Musikwirtschaft und Medien: Märkte - Unternehmen - Strategien*. München, Germany: Verlag Reinhard Fischer.

Seilinger, Gerald (2010a). *Information page of Gerald Seilinger at myspace*. Retrieved 26 October 2010, from http://www.myspace.com/seilinger.

Seilinger, Gerald (2010b). *Interview held by Christine Bauer*. 13 November 2010, Vienna, Austria.

Shiner, Larry E. (2001). *The invention of art: cultural history*. Chicago, Illinois: University of Chicago Press.

Stake, Robert E. (1995). *The Art of Case Study Research*. Thousand Oaks, London, New Delhi: Sage Publications.

Statistik Austria (2007). *Jährliche Personeneinkommen*. Retrieved 23 August 2009, from http://www.statistik.at/web_de/statistiken/soziales/personen-einkommen/jaehrliche_personen_einkommen/index.html.

Stein, Thomas M., Engh, Marcel, & Jakob, Hubert (2008). Bedeutung des Fernsehens für die Musikindustrie: „Pop Idol". In Clement, Michel, Papies, Dominik, & Schusser, Oliver (Eds.), *Ökonomie der Musikindustrie* (pp. 183-194). Wiesbaden, Germany: Gabler.

Stonehouse, George & Pemberton, Jonathan (2002). Strategic planning in SMEs: some empirical findings. *Management Decision, 40*(9), 853-861. doi: 10.1108/00251740210441072.

Strunk, Heinz (2006). Interview with Author Heinz Strunk ("Fleisch ist mein Gemüse"), 20 December 2006. Saarbrücken, Germany.

Swedberg, Richard (2006). The cultural entrepreneur and the creative industries: beginning in Vienna. *Journal of Cultural Economics, 30*(4), 243-261. doi: 10.1007/s10824-006-9016-5.

Throsby, David (2007). Preferred work patterns of creative artists. *Journal of Economics and Finance, 31*(3), 395-402. doi: 10.1007/BF02885729.

Towse, Ruth (1996). *The Economics of Artists' Labour Markets.* Discussion Paper No 3. The Arts Council of England, London, United Kingdom.

Tschmuck, Peter (2003). *Kreativität und Innovation in der Musikindustrie.* Innsbruck, Austria: StudienVerlag.

Tschmuck, Peter (2008). Der Komponist als Unternehmer: Der Wandel der sozioökonomischen Lage der Komponisten im späten 18. Jahrhundert. In Budroni, Paolo (Ed.), *Mozart und Salieri – Partner oder Rivalen?* (pp. 89-96). Vienna, Austria: Vienna University Press.

UNESCO (1980). *Recommendation concerning the Status of the Artist.* United Nations Educational, Scientific and Cultural Organization (UNESCO), Belgrade, Serbia.

van Aken, Joan Ernst (2005). Management Research as a Design Science: Articulating the Research Products of Mode 2 Knowledge Production in Management. *British Journal of Management, 16*, 19-36.

van Bree, Marc (2009). *Orchestras and New Media: A Complete Guide.* Retrieved 10 June 2010, from http://mcmvanbree.com/orchestras_and_new_media.pdf.

VBO (2010). *Information site of the Vienna Ballroom Orchestra (VBO) at Musikergilde.at.* Retrieved 23 September 2010, from http://www.musikergilde.at/index.php?cccpage=visitenkarte_formationen_detail&set_z_m_form=1000&set_z_m_inst=0&set_z_m_data=724.

Viola, Katharina (2009). *Bestandsaufnahme der aktuellen Aus- und Weiterbildungsmöglichkeiten für Kunstschaffende in Hinblick auf Managementskills.* Master's thesis, University of Vienna, Vienna, Austria. Retrieved 20 September 2009 from http://othes.univie.ac.at/3902/1/2009-02-25_0105560.pdf.

Weaver, K. Mark & Bowman, Susan (2005). Entrepreneurship and the arts: Illusion or Reality? Proceeedings of the *USASBE/SBI 2006 Joint Conference*, 12-15 January 2005, Tucson, Arizona.

Weihrich, Heinz (1982). The TOWS matrix: A tool for situational analysis. *Long Range Planning, 15*(2), 54-66. doi: 10.1016/0024-6301(82)90120-0.

White, Stephen A. & Miers, Derek (2008). *BPMN Modeling and Reference Guide: understanding and using BPMN: develop rigorous yet understandable representations of business processes*. Lighthouse Point, Florida: Future Strategies.

Wilde, Thomas & Hess, Thomas (2007). Forschungsmethoden der Wirtschaftsinformatik: Eine empirische Untersuchung. *Wirtschaftsinformatik, 49*(4), 280-287. doi: 10.1007/s11576-007-0064-z.

Wüthrich, Hans A. , Philipp, Andreas F. , & Frentz, Martin H. (1997). *Vorsprung durch Virtualisierung: lernen von virutellen Pionierunternehmen*. Wiesbaden, Germany: Gabler.

Yin, Robert K. (1989). *Case Study Research: Design and Methods* (5th ed.). Newbury Park, California: Sage Publications.

Yin, Robert K. (1993). *Applications of Case Study Research*. Newbury Park, California: Sage Publications.

Appendix

Questionnaire used for the semi-structured interview

Fragen zur Person	*Questions concerning the person*
1.) Was ist Deine Ausbildung?	1.) What is your educational background?
• Hast Du eine Managementausbildung?	• Do you have a management education?
• Woher?	• Where from?
• Wie hast Du Dir Managementskills angeeignet?	• How did you adopt management skills?
2.) Siehst Du Dich als Künstler?	2.) Do you perceive yourself as an artist?
• als Musiker?	• as a musician?
• als Unternehmer?	• as entrepreneur?
• ...	• ...

Expertenfragen	*Expert questions*
3.) Was ist eine Band?	3.) What is a band?
4.) Was ist eine Telefonband? Wie grenzt sie sich von der Band ab?	4.) What is a telephone band? How do you differentiate it from other bands?

Fragen zur Band als Marke	*Questions concerning the band as a brand*
5.) Wie ist die Arbeit des VBO auf folgendem Spektrum einzuschätzen?	5.) How do you rate the work of VBO on following spectrum of characteristics?

Hohe Kunst ----- Kommerz, marktorientiert

6.) Sind die Musiker in der Band austauschbar?

- Warum, warum nicht?

7.) Bist Du austauschbar?

- Warum, warum nicht?

8.) Wie viele Leute sind involviert und wie verteilen sich die Aufgabenbereiche?

9.) Welche Aufgabenbereiche gibt es (noch)?

- Was ist das Besondere am BonbonBall?
- Was ist das Besondere einer Telefon-Big Band?
- Was ist das Besondere an VBO?

Fragen zum Ablauf

10.) Was ist der Start (Kick-Off) für einen Telefonbandauftritt?
11.) Was kommt danach...

- Zu den einzelnen Schritten:
    - Wer?
    - Wann?
    - Wo?
    - Wie?

high arts ----- commerce, market-oriented

6.) Are the musicians in the band exchangeable?

- Why, why not?

7.) Are you exchangeable?

- Why, why not?

8.) How many people are involved, and how are tasks distributed?

9.) What (further) tasks are there?

- What is special about the Bonbon-Ball?
- What is special about a telephone big band?
- What is special about the VBO?

Questions concerning the process

10.) What is the kick-off for the telephone band performance?
11.) What is next...

- Concerning the singe steps:
    - Who?
    - When?
    - Where?
    - How?

103

– Einsatz elektronischer Hilfsmittel?	– Deployment of electronic resources?
– Warum, warum nicht?	– Why, why not?

Spezielle Bereiche	*Special fields*

- Wer startet Auftritt: Anfrage von Veranstalter, Marketing von VBO...?!
- Wie werden Musiker ausgesucht?
- Was kommt zuerst: Zusage zu Veranstalter oder Zusage der Musiker? Von allen, von einem Teil, welcher Teil?
- Gibt es Vertrag mit Musikern? Schriftlich oder mündlich?
- Wie läuft die Verrechnung?
- Wer kümmert sich um Noten?
- Wer transportiert Noten?
- Wer transportiert Equipment?
- Wer übernimmt Aufbau auf Bühne?
- Getränke?
- Koordination der Musiker
- Koordination der Helfer
- Was passiert während des Events?
- Song-Listen für die Verwertungs-

- Who sets off the performance: Enquiry by the organiser, marketing by VBO...?!
- How do you choose the musicians?
- What comes first: acceptance to the organiser or acceptance of the musicians? By all of them, by a part, which part?
- Is there a contract with the musicians? In writing or orally?
- How does compensation work?
- Who handles the sheet music?
- Who transports the sheet music?
- Who transports the equipment?
- Who handles the installation of the stage equipment?
- Beverages?
- Coordination of the musicians
- Coordination of the supporting staff
- What happens during the event?
- Song list for the collecting socie-

gesellschaft?

- Wann ist das Management des Auftritts mit allen Prozessen abgeschlossen?

ty?

- When does the management of the performance with all processes end?

Electronic Business

Herausgegeben von Christine Strauss

Band 1   Rudolf Hartjes: Web Accessibility. Techniken und exemplarische Erfolgsmessung. 2009.

Band 2   Natalia Kryvinska: Converged Network Service Architecture. A Platform for Integrated Services Delivery and Interworking. 2010.

Band 3   Marie-Luise Leitner: Business Impacts of Web Accessibility. A Holistic Approach. 2010.

Band 4   Sonja Höglinger: Barrierefreier Tourismus und die Rolle des Reisemittlers. 2010.

Band 5   Iris C. Rauh: *Online Reputation Mechanisms*. Online-Reputation und deren Management am Beispiel der Hotelindustrie. 2011.

Band 6   Andreas Mladenow / Karl Anton Fröschl: Kooperative Forschung. Eine Intermediäre Perspektive IKT-gestützter Koordinationsmodelle für den universitären Wissens- und Technologietransfer. 2011.

Band 7   Natalia Kryvinska / Christine Strauss: Next Generation Networks – Service Delivery and Management. 2011.

Band 8   Christine Bauer: Bands as Virtual Organisations. Improving the Processes of Band and Event Management with Information and Communication Technologies. 2012.

www.peterlang.de